FOR ALL MY WALKING

Modern Asian Literature

FOR ALL MY WALKING

Translated by Burton Watson

Free-Verse Haiku of Taneda Santōka
with Excerpts from His Diaries

COLUMBIA UNIVERSITY PRESS

NEW YORK

Columbia University Press

Publishers Since 1893

New York   Chichester, West Sussex

Copyright © 2003 Columbia University Press

All rights reserved

Library of Congress Cataloging-in-Publication Data

Taneda, Santoka, 1882–1940.

    [Poems. English. Selections]

    For all my walking : free-verse haiku of

Taneda Santoka with excerpts from his diaries /

translated by Burton Watson.

        p.   cm.—(Modern Asian literature series)

    ISBN 978-0-231-12516-1 (cloth : alk. paper)

    ISBN 978-0-231-12517-8 (paper : alk. paper)

    I. Watson, Burton, 1925–   II. Taneda,

Santoka, 1882–1940. Nikki. English. Selections.

III. Title.   IV. Series.

∞

Columbia University Press books are printed on

permanent and durable acid-free paper.

Printed in the United States of America

Contents

Chronology of the Life of Taneda Santōka

1882   DECEMBER 3. Born in Nishisabaryō, Yamaguchi
       Prefecture

1892   Mother commits suicide

1902   Enters Department of Literature at Waseda
       University in Tokyo

1904   Withdraws from Waseda and returns to
       Nishisabaryō

1906   Father goes into sake-brewing business

1909   Marries Satō Sakino of neighboring village

1910   Son, Ken, is born

1913   Becomes follower of Ogiwara Seisensui
       Begins publishing free-style haiku in *Sōun*
       (*Layered Clouds*)

1916   Sake brewery fails
       With wife and child, moves to Kumamoto,
       in Kyushu

1918   Younger brother, Jirō, commits suicide
       Grandmother dies

1919   Goes to Tokyo alone and works at various jobs

1920   At request of wife's family, is divorced from wife

1921   Father dies

1923   After Great Kanto Earthquake, returns to
       Kumamoto

1924   Attempts suicide (?) by standing in front of trolley,
       and is put under the care of Mochizuki Gian, a
       priest of Zen temple Hōon-ji in Kumamoto

1925	Becomes ordained Zen priest and is put in charge of Mitori Kannon-dō
1926	Sets off on three-year walking trip through Kyushu, Honshu, Shikoku, and Shodōjima
1929	Returns to Kumamoto, but sets off on more walking trips
1932	Moves into small cottage called Gochū-an in Ogōri, Yamaguchi Prefecture
1933–1938	Lives in cottage, supported by friends; takes occasional trips; and publishes several small collections of poems
1938	Late in year, moves to Yuda, Yamaguchi Prefecture
1939	Takes walking trip in Shikoku Late in year, moves to cottage in Matsuyama, in Shikoku
1940	APRIL. Publishes collection of poems, *Sōmokutō* (*Grass and Tree Stupa*) OCTOBER 11. Dies in sleep in cottage in Matsuyama

FOR ALL MY WALKING

Introduction

The brief poetic form known today as haiku enjoyed immense popularity in Japan during the Edo period (1600–1867), when poets such as Bashō and Buson produced superlative works in the genre and a craze for haiku writing spread through many sectors of the population. But by the time of the Meiji Restoration in 1868, the beginning of Japan's modern era, the form had sunk to a very low level of literary worth, being marked mainly by stale imitations of the past or facile wordplay or satire, often of a vulgar nature.

In the early years of the Meiji period, the poet and critic Masaoka Shiki (1867–1902) succeeded in injecting new life into the form and restoring it as a vehicle for serious artistic expression. Since his time, the writing of haiku has constituted an integral part of the Japanese literary scene, and in recent years the form has been taken up by poets in many other countries and languages as well.

Although Shiki greatly broadened the subject matter of the haiku and employed a more colloquial diction, he continued to write in the traditional form, which uses seventeen syllables or sound symbols arranged in a 5–7–5 pattern and invariably includes a *kigo* (season word) that indicates the particular season in which the poem is set.

Shiki had two outstanding disciples in the art of haiku composition: Takahama Kyoshi (1874–1959) and Kawahigashi Hekigotō (1873–1937). Kyoshi, writing in the traditional haiku form as Shiki had, produced during his long life a large body of works that has been highly esteemed by Japanese critics. Hekigotō, on the contrary, in time grew dissatisfied with the formal requirements of the traditional haiku and began experimenting with the writing of what are now known as free-verse or free-style haiku, brief poems that do not adhere to the 5–7–5 sound pattern and do not regularly include a season word.

This new free-style haiku form was originated by one of Hekigotō's disciples, Ogiwara Seisensui (1884–1976). And Taneda Santōka, whose free-style haiku are the subject of this volume, was a disciple of Seisensui. Thus, in the kinship terms so beloved by Japanese critics, Taneda Santōka was a literary grandson of Kawahigashi Hekigotō and a great-grandson of Masaoka Shiki.

Although Santōka wrote conventional-style haiku in his youth, the vast majority of his works, and those for which he is most admired, are in free-verse form. He also left a number of diaries in which he frequently records the circumstances that led to the composition of a particular poem or group of poems. His poetry attracted only limited notice during his lifetime, but in recent years in Japan there has been a remarkable upsurge of interest in his life and writings. His complete works were published in seven large volumes in 1972 and 1973,[1] and Japanese bookstores now customarily display an impressive array of Santōka's poems, letters, and diaries, as well as critical studies and memoirs by persons who knew him.

As Ivan Morris noted some years ago in *The Nobility of Failure: Tragic Heroes in the History of Japan,* the Japanese have a marked fondness for people who in one way or another have made a mess of their lives. And, as we will see when we come to a discussion of Santōka's biography, he was a prime example of the "messy" type. Much of the popularity that his

1. *Teihon Santōka Zenshū* (hereafter cited as *ZS*) (Tokyo: Shun'yū-dō, 1972–1973).

works now enjoy is due to their undoubted literary worth, but much of it is also attributable to the highly unconventional and in some ways tragic life he led. His poetry and his life demand to be taken together.

Taneda Santōka, whose childhood name was Shōichi, was born on December 3, 1882, the elder son of a well-to-do landowner in Nishisabaryō, in what is now part of Hōfu City in Yamaguchi Prefecture. He had two sisters and a younger brother. His father seems to have been a rather weak-willed man who spent his time dabbling in local politics, chasing after women, and in general dissipating the family fortune, which had been of considerable size at the time he fell heir to it.

When Santōka was eleven by Japanese reckoning, his mother committed suicide by throwing herself down the family well. Santōka, who was playing with companions in a nearby outbuilding, heard the ensuing commotion. Although efforts were made to bar him from the scene, he managed to squeeze through the legs of the bystanders and reach the well just as his mother's lifeless body was lifted out of it. The trauma inflicted by what he saw haunted him to the end of his life.

Just what drove his mother to such action is unknown, though presumably it was despair at her husband's dissipation; at least that appears to have been Santōka's view of the matter. Thereafter, he was raised by his grandmother.

After completing the equivalent of a high-school education in Yamaguchi, he entered the Department of Literature at Waseda University in Tokyo in the fall of 1902. He had already shown a marked interest in literature and had begun writing conventional-style haiku. It was at this time that he adopted the literary name Santōka, which means

"Mountaintop Fire." The name has no literary connotations, but derives from a Chinese system of divination known in Japanese as *natchin*.

Having failed to fulfill the first-year requirements, Santōka withdrew from the university in early 1904. Nervous breakdown was given as the reason for his departure, though this may have been largely a euphemism for the alcoholism that was to plague him throughout his life. In any event, his father by this time was in such financial straits that he could no longer afford to pay for his son's schooling, and Santōka returned to Nishisabaryō.

With little experience and profoundly poor judgment, Santōka's father decided to sell some of the family property and buy a brewery devoted to the making of sake, or Japanese rice wine. Santōka was to assist him in managing the business. In hopes that marriage would help settle him down, a match was arranged between Santōka and a young woman from a nearby village. The couple were married in 1909, and the following year a son, Ken, was born. But it soon became apparent that Santōka was not fit for married life, or for the running of a sake brewery, for that matter. In 1916, because of inept management and the failure of the sake, for two years in a row, to be of marketable quality, the brewery went bankrupt. Santōka's father fled into hiding, and Santōka and his wife and child moved to Kumamoto in Kyushu, where the wife opened a small store that sold picture frames.

Santōka's younger brother, Jirō, had been adopted into another family, but the adoption was annulled at the time of the Taneda family's business failure. Left in Yamaguchi to face the debts from the bankruptcy, with no help coming from Santōka, he hanged himself in 1918. The same year, Santōka's grandmother, who had raised him after his mother's death, died in Yamaguchi in highly straightened circumstances.

These two deaths were to weigh heavily on Santōka's already troubled mind.

In 1919 Santōka left his wife and son and went to Tokyo. There he worked briefly for a cement company, quit that job, took another job with a library, but eventually quit that as well. His failure to stick to anything was once again attributed to "nervous disability." Meanwhile, his wife's family pressed him to agree to a divorce, which he did in 1920. The following year, his father died. On September 1, 1923, the Great Kanto Earthquake destroyed the building in Tokyo where he had been lodging, and he returned to Kumamoto penniless. His former wife obligingly let him assist her in the picture-frame store.

In December 1924, Santōka, drunk, one night stationed himself in front of an oncoming trolley, his arms raised in an attitude of defiance. Whether this was a serious attempt at suicide or merely a drunken stunt, no one knows. In any event, the trolley screeched to a halt, and Santōka was saved. Instead of being handed over to the police, he was taken to Hōon-ji, a temple of the Sōtō Zen sect in Kumamoto, where the head priest, Mochizuki Gian, in a signal display of Buddhist compassion, agreed to take him in and see what could be done with him.

This event marks the end of what might be termed act 1 in the Santōka drama. In act 2, things in some ways take a very different turn. Few of the poems in the selection that follows date from this initial period, though some refer to the persons or events of that time. As early as 1913, Santōka had begun writing free-style haiku and sending them to *Soun* (*Layered Clouds*), the haiku magazine published by Ogiwara Seisensui. But the poems for which he is now admired and on which his reputation rests were written in the period that followed.

Under Mochizuki Gian's direction, Santōka took up the study of Buddhism and began practicing Zen meditation. In 1925, when he was forty-four by Japanese reckoning, he was ordained a priest of the Sōtō Zen sect. His first assignment was as caretaker of the Mitori Kannon-dō, a small Buddhist hall situated near Kumamoto that enshrined a figure of the bodhisattva Kannon. In addition to looking after the hall and ringing the bell morning and evening, he went on begging trips in the neighborhood.

In April 1926, he left this assignment and set off on the first of his many walking trips, journeys in which he tramped literally thousands of miles through the Japanese countryside. It is uncertain just what impelled him to embark on these wanderings. Such journeys were often part of the religious training of Buddhist monks, particularly those of the Zen school, and Santōka may have felt that this was the type of religious practice that suited him best. At the same time, walking trips had helped provide literary inspiration to such eminent poets of the past as Saigyō and Bashō, and Santōka clearly found that the constant change of scene greatly aided his poetic powers. The two activities of walking and composing haiku seemed to complement each other, and his many journeys, lonely and wearisome as they were, gave him a sense of fulfillment that he could gain in no other way.

On such trips, Santōka wore the traditional garb of a mendicant monk—a black robe and a broad coolie-type hat to keep off the sun and rain—and carried a wooden staff. Begging for alms was, of course, a traditional part of the monastic life in many branches of Buddhism in the past, and it continues to be widely practiced. It has two purposes. One is to provide material support for the monastic community, thus allowing the monks to devote greater time to religious activities. The other is to give members of the lay community an opportunity to gain religious merit by donating food, clothing, or money to the monastic order.

Zen monks in Japan customarily conduct such *takuhatsu* (begging expeditions) in a group, with the name of the temple with which they are affiliated or where they are undergoing training plainly written on their alms bag so that donors will know where their contributions are going. Santōka, it should be noted, carried out his begging trips strictly on his own and had no temple name on his alms bag, which put him at a distinct disadvantage. He refers to his activities by the term *gyōkotsu* (itinerant begging), and it is clear from his diaries that he was at times stopped by the police for questioning and regarded as little more than a common beggar.

When begging for alms, monks customarily station themselves in front of a house or store and chant a religious text. If they are lucky, someone then comes out of the building and deposits rice, vegetables, or money in their alms bag or begging bowl. Often, however, there is no response, or only a brusque word of refusal, in which case the mendicants move on to the next building.

On any given day, Santōka usually continued to beg until he had enough in the way of donations to cover the day's expenses. These included the price of a night's lodging at an inexpensive flophouse-type inn and enough sake or *shōchū*, a cheap liquor usually made from sweet potatoes, to ensure a good night's rest.

On the first of his walking trips, Santōka was away from Kumamoto for a total of three years. He spent part of the time visiting temples in the island of Shikoku to pray for the repose of his mother's spirit. He also visited the smaller island of Shodōjima, where he paid his respects at the grave of Ozaki Hōsai (1885–1926). Hōsai, like Santōka, had been a

writer of free-style haiku and a leading contributor to Ogi-
wara Seisensui's poetry magazine. He had died in poverty in
Shodōjima in 1926.[2] Santōka returned to Kumamoto in
1929, but soon set off again on further wanderings.

In 1932, weary of the hardships of itinerant life, he at-
tempted to acquire a small *an* (hermitage) in Kawatana, a
hot-springs town in northern Kyushu that had greatly taken
his fancy. But he was apparently too much of an oddity for
the local inhabitants to stomach, and his plans got nowhere.
Instead, through the help of friends, in late September he set-
tled in a small cottage in Ogōri, near his birthplace in Yam-
aguchi Prefecture. He named it the Gochū-an, from a pas-
sage in chapter 25 of the Lotus Sutra that praises the saving
power of the bodhisattva Kannon.

During the years when Santōka was living in the Gochū-
an, and later in Yuda and Matsuyama, he went on few beg-
ging expeditions and was almost wholly dependent for his
daily needs on contributions from friends in the neighbor-
hood and more distant patrons or on money sent to him by
his son, Ken. For his meals, he relied mainly on vegetables
from his garden or edible wild plants, but because of lack of
funds he often ran out of such staples as rice, soy sauce, and
bean paste, to say nothing of sake and tobacco. He endured
these periods of privation as best he could, going with little
or no food for days at a time, but they hardly contributed to
his emotional stability or peace of mind. As is evident from
his diaries, he was ashamed to be so reliant on others, but at

2. For translations of a number of Ozaki Hōsai's haiku, along
with an introductory essay on his life and poetry, see *Right Under
the Big Sky, I Don't Wear a Hat: The Haiku and Prose of Hōsai Ozaki*,
trans. Hiroaki Sato (Berkeley, Calif.: Stone Bridge Press, 1993).

the same time determined that, whatever the conventional judgment of his way of life might be, he would continue to concentrate on his haiku writing.

Santōka remained in the Gochū-an until 1938, when the building, already in a dilapidated state, became totally unfit for habitation. He moved to temporary quarters in nearby Yuda Hot Springs, and at the end of the following year settled in a cottage in Matsuyama City in Shikoku.

By the time he moved to Matsuyama, he had published a number of collections of his poems and had many friends in poetry circles. On October 10, 1940, a group of friends gathered at his cottage in Matsuyama for the type of poetry meeting they often held there, but, finding Santōka too drunk to participate in the proceedings, they moved to another location. When they looked in on him the following day, they discovered that he had died in his sleep. He was fifty-eight at the time, or fifty-nine by Japanese reckoning.

Writing of himself in later life, Santōka said: "Talentless and incompetent as I am, there are two things I can do, and two things only: walk, with my own two feet; compose, composing my poems."[3] Sometimes on his walking trips, he visited famous shrines or temples or passed through the larger cities, but much of the time he was traveling over country roads, often in quite remote areas. In his younger days, if he was tired and drunk enough when night fell, he would simply bed down in a nearby field—he called it "sleeping with the crickets"—though usually he put up at a cheap inn. On his last begging trip in 1939, however, when Japan was already at war and few people were in the mood to give alms

3. Diary, August 27, 1940, *ZS*, vol. 6, p. 53.

to a dubious beggar-monk, he often had to spend the night in whatever makeshift shelter he could find along the road. One of the few real pleasures of such walking trips, referred to frequently in his poems, were the hot baths he took in inns, public baths, or hot springs. They not only eased the pain and fatigue of day-after-day tramping, but helped greatly to raise his spirits.

Over the years, he made a number of friends through his literary activities, and he often visited them in the course of his travels and took part in meetings on haiku writing. His friends seem to have welcomed such visits, no doubt because they admired his poetry and found him congenial company, though at times he rather abused their hospitality. When he was on the road, he sent them postcards and arranged to get mail from them at towns along his route.

As is evident from his diaries, Santōka was subject to widely fluctuating moods. Often he records his delight with the mountain and seaside scenery he encountered on his journeys, or mentions his pleasure at happening on an inn with good food and clean bedding, particularly if he was lucky enough to have a room to himself. On most occasions, he had to share a room with various other travelers—pilgrims or pseudo-pilgrims, craftsmen, itinerant peddlers (the last often from Korea or Taiwan, areas that were at this time under Japanese control). In his diaries, he customarily notes the name of the inn where he stayed and the price of a night's lodging and assigns it a rating—good, middling, or poor—depending on the accommodations and atmosphere of the place.

At times he applauds the kindness of the keepers of the cheap inns he stayed in, the worldly wise ramblings of his fellow travelers, and the enjoyment he derived from drinking with them. But at other times he finds his companions merely irritating, complains of the innkeeper's noisy children, or rails at the dirt and squalor of his surroundings. And at times he seems incapable of anything but endless harping on his loneliness, his immoderate drinking and the injury it does to his health, and the failure and hypocrisy of his attempts to live the life of a Buddhist monk. From a mood of elation he sinks into an all-but-suicidal despair.

And out of this emotional turmoil, these recurrent binges and periods of self-reproof, come the poems, many thousands of them, preserved in his published collections and in his diaries and other writings. Their imagery is often that of the scenes he encountered on his trips, particularly those in the countryside. But these are not *shasei* (sketches from life), such as Masaoka Shiki wrote and recommended to other poets. Like Bashō, Santōka believed that the poet and the scene he or she observes should fuse with each other until they become a single entity. The primary purpose of the poem is not to describe the scene, but to convey the inner feelings of the writer. As Santōka himself noted, "Through nature I sing of myself."[4] His poems, for all their naturalistic imagery, are first of all portrayals of the poet's constantly shifting moods and emotional states.

Santōka's free-style haiku employ a variety of syntactic patterns, and their language is almost always the colloquial speech of modern Japan, with occasional touches of local dialect. Unlike most traditional Japanese poetry, they make no use of allusion, wordplay, or literary embellishment. Nor should readers look in them for any clever displays of wit or arresting imagery; in most cases, it is the very everyday-ness of the scenes or feelings depicted that is the point.

4. Diary, April 4, 1935, *ZS*, vol. 4, p. 193.

Since free-style haiku do not observe the conventional seventeen-syllable pattern, they may vary considerably in length. Ogiwara Seisensui, Santōka's mentor, stated that the free-style haiku should be of "a length that can be read out in one breath." Judging from his own poems in the form and his critical remarks, this for him meant a length of between six and around twenty-eight syllables. He also said that the poem should include a caesura, or "major break" in the rhythm.[5] Santōka's free-style haiku in general conform to these specifications, though many of them have no marked caesura.

Santōka frequently concludes a poem with an image drawn from the natural world, appending it to the end of the poem without any indication of just how it is meant to relate to what has gone before. We see this pattern in one of his most famous works, composed in 1926, when he set off on the first of his walking trips:

the deeper I go   wakeitte mo
the deeper I go   wakeitte mo
green mountains   aoi yama

Here it is clear that what he is venturing deeper and deeper into, at least on the literal level of the poem, are the green mountains of the Japanese countryside. The verb he employs, *wakeiru*, however, suggests someone pushing or forcing his way through a dense and resisting mass: the green mountains, the poem implies, are perhaps not as pleasant or as passable as they seemed from a distance, and there is a hint that the traveler may in fact never come out on the other side.

5. Makoto Ueda, *Modern Japanese Poets and the Nature of Literature* (Stanford, Calif.: Stanford University Press, 1983), pp. 318–20.

Moreover, we sense that, as so often in Buddhist-oriented literature, the journey through the physical landscape is at the same time a mental and spiritual probing into the inner self. As the Zen Master Jakushitsu Genkō (1290–1367) said to one of his students, "You are the green mountain, the green mountain is you." Incidentally, although the poem undoubtedly refers to Santōka's own experience, because of the absence of an expressed subject in the original, the opening lines could as well be translated as "the deeper you go" or "the deeper one goes."

The poem is, of course, also noteworthy because of its use of repetition. In a form as brief as the haiku, it might seem foolish to take up space by merely repeating what has been said, yet here the repetition works splendidly.

The following poem, written in 1938 when Santōka visited the village of Nishisabaryō in Yamaguchi Prefecture, where he was born, ends, like the preceding one, with an image from the natural world:

nothing left of the house	umareta ie wa
I was born in	atokata mo nai
fireflies	hōtaru

Here the relationship between the first part of the poem and the image that concludes it is less obvious. Fireflies in Japan are associated with damp spots overgrown with weeds or other vegetation, and in this poem they most likely are intended to indicate the neglect and desolation of the site where Santōka's once prosperous home stood. At the same time, the darting, wavering lights of the fireflies may be meant to suggest the disembodied spirits of Santōka's departed parents and kin, who—like the *hitodama* (will-o'-the-wisps) of Japanese folklore—continue to hover about the spot. *Hōtaru*, it may be noted, is a variant pronunciation of the standard Japanese word *hotaru*.

There is no question of the exact nature of the image with which the following poem concludes:

valiantly—that too	isamashiku mo
pitifully—that too	kanashiku mo
white boxes	shiroi hako

In 1937 war broke out between Japan and China, and the poem is one of several written the following year, when Santōka was viewing the cremated remains of Japanese soldiers killed in action in China as they were brought home to grieving relatives in small boxes wrapped in white cloth.[6] The poem's ambiguity lies not in the image of the white boxes but in the adverbs that precede it, here shorn of the verb or verbs that they were presumably intended to modify. Do they refer to the actions of the soldiers who met death in a foreign land? Or to the solemn return of the boxes to Japan, perhaps to the accompaniment of martial music or a patriotic speech or two? Or are they meant to sum up the whole series of actions in which the dead men and their families, obeying the command of the leaders of wartime Japan, attempted to do what they knew was expected of them?

Ellipsis of this kind is, of course, a common enough technique in haiku, one whose use would seem almost inevitable, given the brevity of the form. But in poems such as the one just quoted, Santōka employs it in novel ways, fragmenting the syntax and creating gaps in meaning in a manner that challenges the ingenuity of the reader. In such poems, what is said is often of less importance than what is *not* said.

6. See the diary excerpt for July 11, 1938, p. 93.

In the last example to be presented here, written in 1939 when Santōka was in Shikoku on his last extended walking trip, the image—the autumn wind—appears at the beginning rather than the end of the poem, setting the somber mood for what follows:

autumn wind   aki kaze
for all my walking—   aruite mo
for all my walking—   aruite mo

In Santōka's writings, "walking" designates not only the mere fact of journeying on foot, but a kind of religious practice aimed at achieving a higher degree of understanding and acceptance. For all his endless walking, the poem suggests, that goal continues to elude the poet.

Because Santōka writes in free-verse form, he can employ a much wider variety of poem lengths, rhythms, and syntactic patterns than someone working in the traditional haiku form, and can perhaps achieve a greater range of poetic effects. But because of the very formlessness of the free style, it is at times difficult to say whether what he has produced is in fact a real poem or merely snippets of language strung out on the page.

Perhaps this does not really matter. Santōka had a certain conception of what his haiku, whether long or short, should sound like, what kind of mood they should evoke. Readers will note, for example, how often certain images recur: the dragonfly, the crow, the bad tooth, the persimmon tree, the drizzly autumn rain—this last perhaps because he was obliged to tramp through it rather than merely contemplate it from a comfortably sheltered spot, as so many other poets have done.

Santōka made little effort to broaden his haiku style; did not, like so many of his contemporaries, engage in controversy over the proper nature of haiku; and did not comment at length on the haiku of other writers. Instead, he worked to create poems that were distinctively his own—spare, stark, simple in expression—tirelessly revising earlier works and experimenting with different ways of handling the themes and images that most interested him.

Aware of his abundant shortcomings, he stated, as we have seen, that there were only two things he could do well: walk and write poems. About his walking, no more need be said. But that in his difficult later years he continued to labor away at his poems seems to me deserving of great respect. From a life marked otherwise largely by failure, he managed to salvage something of real value. Giving the last poem quoted a more positive interpretation, we might say that for all his walking he has in fact something very solid to show— the poems

In 1980 John Stevens published *Mountain Tasting: Zen Haiku by Santōka Taneda*, which contains translations of 372 of Santōka's haiku, along with a lengthy introduction on his life and poetry. Stevens, who teaches at a Japanese university and is an ordained priest of the Sōtō Zen sect, pays special attention to Santōka's life as a Zen monk and the poems that reflect what Stevens regards as the Zen aspects of his work. In my own selection of 245 haiku, I have tried as much as possible to avoid duplicating Stevens's work, though this has not always proved possible with Santōka's most famous poems.

My own interest in Santōka's work centers more on the poetry itself, particularly the manner in which it experiments with different poem lengths and syntactic patterns, and the challenge that these present to the translator. Since free-style haiku do not adhere to the conventional 5–7–5 sound pattern, the translator is free to break them more or less wherever he or she wants or, like Hiroaki Sato in his translations of Ozaki Hōsai's free-style haiku, to translate them as a single line in English. I have regularly broken my own translations into two or three lines in the hope that this division will help readers grasp the syntax of the poem and slow down the reading.

Modern Japanese in nearly all cases requires more syllables or sound symbols to express a given idea or image than does modern English, and so English translations of Japanese haiku, if not deliberately padded, will almost inevitably turn out to be briefer in wording than the originals. And when confronted with a poem such as Santōka's haiku "oto wa shigure ka," one comes out with something looking like this:

> that sound
> the rain?

Can an utterance as brief as this be called a poem? I leave it to readers to decide.

In April 1940, six months before his death, Santōka compiled and published a selection of his haiku written over the preceding fifteen years. Titled *Sōmokutō* (*Grass and Tree Stupa*), it contains 701 haiku that he felt represented his best work. In my translations, I have indicated poems drawn from this collection by adding the letters *SMT* at the end of the transliterated versions of the poems. I have arranged the poems by year of composition, in nearly all cases following the dating indicated in the seven volumes of Santōka's collected works (*Teihon Santōka Zenshū*), though there is controversy regarding the exact dating of certain poems.

After Santōka set out on his first walking trip in 1926, he kept diaries of his daily activities. He burned the diaries from this first trip, but those from his later years, beginning in September 1930 and continuing, with only minor gaps, to the time of his death, are extant and have been published in *Tei-hon Santōka Zenshū*. Customarily he noted the weather; his activities, including what he ate and drank; the friends he visited or who visited him; and the flowers and birds he saw around him. In addition, he often commented on his state of mind and the progress of his work. After these observations, he usually recorded the haiku he had composed that day or the revisions he had made in earlier poems. When he was on a walking trip, he usually noted the distance he had covered during the day, the amount of rice and money he had received from his begging, and his daily expenses.

I have included fairly lengthy excerpts from his early diaries to indicate their nature and the type of life Santōka experienced on his begging expeditions. From the later diaries, which tend to be gloomy and repetitious, I have selected a few passages that throw light on his poems and his outlook in general.

The originals of the poems are given in romanized form so that readers may observe the subtle variations in syntax and the pleasing sound effects that characterize many of them— for example, the original of poem 201 in my selection:

yama no shizukesa e shizuka naru ame

Since such sound effects and subtleties of syntax can seldom be reproduced adequately in English, I have in my translations concentrated on bringing across as accurately as possible the imagery and emotional impact of the poems.

POEMS AND DIARY ENTRIES

Taishō 3 (1914)

1

cloudless sky
peer through a glass of hard liquor
that deep color!

Taishō 4 (1915)

2

wind from the sea
butterflies in embankment weeds
never resting

Taishō 6 (1917)

3

husband and wife quarreling
night
spiders dangle down

4

so still the street
big hole
dug in it

1 sora ni kumo nashi sakashimiru kashu no kōki iro yo
2 kaze ga umi yori dotegusa no chōchō ochitsukazu
3 isakaeru fūfu ni yoru kumo sagari keri
4 ōkina ana ga horaruru machi no shizukesa yo

Taishō 7 (1918)

5

whiteness of the rice
red of pickled plum
these treasures!

Taishō 9 (1920)

6

come home
in falling snow
write my wife a letter

Taishō 15 (1926)

7

the deeper I go
the deeper I go
green mountains

8

wet to the skin
the stone here
pointing out the path

5 meshi no shirosa no umeboshi no akasa tōtōkere
6 yuki furu naka o kaeri kite tsuma e tegami kaku
7 wakeitte mo wakeitte mo aoi yama (SMT)
8 shitodo ni nurete kore wa michishirube no ishi (SMT)

9
blazing sky above me
walking
begging

Shōwa 2–3 (1927–1928)
10
bush clover!
pampas grass!
I'm coming through

11
wobbly on my feet
the good taste
of water

12
watching the moon
go down
me alone

9 enten o itadaite koiaruku (SMT)
10 fumiwakeru hagi yo susuki yo (SMT)
11 hyōhyō to shite mizu o ajiwau (SMT)
12 ochikakaru tsuki o mite iru ni hitori (SMT)

13
this body
still alive
scratching it

14
reflection
in the water
a traveler

15
happily drunk
tree leaves
drifting down

16
road running
straight ahead
lonely

17
letting a dragonfly
sit on my hat
walking along

13 ikinokotta karada kaite iru (SMT)
14 mizu ni kage aru tabibito de aru (SMT)
15 horo-horo yōte ko no ha furu (SMT)
16 massugu na michi de samishii (SMT)
17 kasa ni tombo o tomarasete aruku (SMT)

18
I go on walking
higan lilies
go on blooming*

Higanbana (equinox flower), also called
manjushage, is a wild lily that blooms around
the autumn equinox.

Shōwa 4 (1929)
19
slipped
fell down
mountains are silent

20
legs worn out
a dragonfly
lights on them

21
inside the newly mended
paper panels
alone

18 arukitsuzukeru higanbana sakitsuzukeru (*SMT*)
19 subette koronde yama ga hissori (*SMT*)
20 tsukareta ashi e tombo tomatta (*SMT*)
21 harikaeta shōji no naka no hitori (*SMT*)

22
front, back
weight of baggage
I can't throw off

Shōwa 5 (1930)
23
hurry down the road
never look back

24
in the shade of the rock
sure to be
water bubbling up

25
rain dumped
from that cloud
getting wet in it

26
has my hat too
sprung a leak?

22 sutekirenai nimotsu no omosa mae ushiro (SMT)
23 furikaeranai michi o isogu
24 iwakage masashiku mizu ga waite iru (SMT)
25 ano kumo ga otoshita ame ni nurete iru (SMT)
26 kasa mo moridashita ka (SMT)

27
my monk's robe
all torn like this
grass seeds

28
so drunk
I slept
with the crickets!

29
warm
the straw matting
someone spread over me

30
no help
for the likes of me
I go on walking

31
I cross
a river
that's all dried up

27 koromo konna ni yaburete kusa no mi (*SMT*)
28 yōte kōrogi to nete ita yo (*SMT*)
29 donata ka kakete kudasatta mushiro atatakashi
30 dō shō mo nai watashi ga aruite iru
31 karekitta kawa o wataru (*SMT*)

32
there were hands
to scratch
the itchy places

33
morning bath
soaking in the stillness
of hot water brimming over

34
more houses
deeper in the mountain?
he's got an ox in tow

35
falling away behind me
mountains I'll never see again

36
now they're burned
these are all the ashes
from my diaries?*

*Santōka burned the diaries from his first trip because
he was ashamed of what he had written.

32 kayui tokoro o kaku te ga atta
33 afururu asayu no shizukesa ni hitaru
34 mada oku ni ie ga aru ushi o hiite yuku
35 mata miru koto mo nai yama ga tōzakaru (SMT)
36 yakisutete nikki no hai no kore dake ka

37
men and women in the bath
shouting back and forth
over the partition

38
gleam
of the 1-sen coin
tossed my way*

*The sen, a coin no longer in use, was worth
one-hundredth the value of the yen.

39
curt unfriendly woman
body big
in late pregnancy

40
one water pipe
leads off from the stream
lone house in autumn

41
dipped up
moonlit water
drank my fill

37 kabe o hedatete yu no naka no danjo sazamekiau
38 nageataerareta issen no hikari da
39 sugenai onna wa ōkiku harande ita
40 hitosuji no mizu o hiki hitotsuya no aki
41 tsuki no mizu o kumiagete nomitatta

42
peaceful in mind
getting up   going to bed
in mountains

43
a little bit feverish
hurrying in the wind

44
sleep on the ground
sooner or later
peaceful as a clod of dirt

45
to the sound
of flowing water
found my way down to the village

46
not a cloud in sight
off comes my hat

42 kokoro shizuka ni yama no okifushi
43 sukoshi netsu ga aru kaze no naka o isogu
44 izure wa tsuchikure no yasukesa de tsuchi ni neru
45 mizuoto to issho ni sato e kudarite kita (SMT)
46 mattaku kumo ga nai kasa o nugi (SMT)

September 9, 1930. Off on another trip. . . . Once more I come to realize that in fact I'm nothing but a beggar-monk, and so I start out on another journey. . . . I'll walk as far as I can walk, go as far as I can go.

47
clear bright morning
straw sandals
feel just right*

*Waraji (straw sandals) are the usual footwear of monks on begging trips, though Santōka often wore cloth jika-tabi, the split-toed footgear worn by workmen, because they were cheaper and lasted longer.

48
sound of waves
far off   close by
how much longer to live?

49
not a scrap of cloud in it
sky lonelier than ever

50
at times
I stop begging
looking at mountains

47 karari to hareta asa no waraji mo shikkuri
48 namioto tōku nari chikaku nari yomei ikubaku zo
49 hitokire no kumo mo nai sora no sabishisa masaru
50 aruiwa kou koto o yame yama o mite iru (SMT)

September 16, 1930 [on a walking trip in northern Kyushu]. Cloudy, drizzle. Begging in the town of Hitoyoshi. Miyakawa Inn, 35 sen, good.*

I was very patient again today. My begging conduct was not all that bad, though I hit on occasional snags. Despite some unpleasant moments, I managed not to lose my temper.

Hitoyoshi has lots of inns, eateries, drinking places, and everywhere you look, women who appear to be prostitutes. All quite pushy, but on the other hand more generous with their money than ordinary people. When I find myself gratefully accepting a 1-sen copper coin from these women, with their powder-stained faces and disheveled look, I can only pray for their happiness. You've had bad luck, but soon I hope you'll take up with some man you care about and get a little fun out of living!

Things are lonely tonight—in the big upstairs room, just two of us, a young Korean candy peddler and myself. He's an unusually quiet type, very congenial. From these itinerant peddlers who go around the countryside I hear about the miserable lot of the local farming families. . . .

A day laborer sweating from morning to evening, if a man, may make 80 sen; if a woman, 50 sen. A charcoal maker working all day will make 25 sen at most; someone fishing as efficiently as possible in the Kuma River (famous for its sweetfish) may get 70 or 80 sen for one day's catch. Obviously, these people are just barely staying alive. They're certainly not enjoying life. When I think of it, the life I live is way better than I deserve.

*These are Santōka's notations on the name of the inn where he stayed, the price of a night's lodging, and his rating of its quality.

September 20, 1930. Westerners try to conquer the mountains. People of the East contemplate the mountains. For us, mountains are not an object of scientific study but a work of art. Patiently I taste the mountains.

51
no more houses
to beg from
clouds on the mountain

52
windy night
a sound of tapping
at the door

53
autumn
already reddening
the leaves of the mountain sumac

54
I don't care
if it *does* rain—
it rains

51 mono kou ie mo naku nari yama ni wa kumo (*SMT*)
52 kaze no yo no to o tataku oto ga aru
53 aki wa ichihayaku yama no haze o some
54 furu mo yokarō ame ga furu

October 1, 1930. Today as I was walking along, I kept thinking to myself: when there are trains, when there are automobiles, to walk, and moreover to walk in straw sandals—what an outmoded, what an inefficient and burdensome way to travel! As a matter of fact, on the road today there were autos and bicycles passing from time to time, but I met almost no one who was walking. Nevertheless, by venturing to do something so ludicrous, I, who am not very clever, justify my existence.

October 17, 1930. Cloudy, later clearing. Resting for health reasons. Inn the same as last night.

Last night couldn't get to sleep until twelve. Perhaps because I overexerted myself. Perhaps because of the potato *shōchū* I drank. Perhaps because I'm coming down with a cold. Hips and legs feverish, tired, achy, painful. In my soup at breakfast I put some of the red pepper I got in my begging last night. As I grow older, I find myself more and more favoring foods that are hot, strong-smelling, bitter, puckery. . . . Mental and physical condition anything but good, still I made myself get up and get out of the inn by eight. I intended to do my usual begging, but I had a fever and felt so awful I knew that was impossible. So when I finally happened on a little shrine building by the side of the road, I lay down on the narrow wooden platform. While I was lying there, four or five children from the neighborhood appeared and began saying something. When I looked, I saw they had spread some matting on the ground and were telling me to lie down on that. Thank you very much!

Burning with fever and much under the weather, I stretched out on the matting. Not dreaming, but not really awake either, I lay there drowsing for two hours or so when I discovered that my legs were no longer shaky and I could speak in a normal voice. So I went on begging for two hours more. In the last house I stopped at, I ran into a very patient old woman, so I recited the *Shushōgi* and the Kannon Sutra.[*] And in the course of reciting these, I began to feel much better in both mind and body.

> 55
> chill chill of earth
> I give up
> my feverish body to it

55 daichi hiebie to shite netsu no aru karada o makasu

I went back to the inn where I stayed last night and lay down in bed. I drank some water (the water here is very good, very tasty), and I thought, if I just take things easy, I can get back into shape. As I had hoped, by evening I felt venturesome enough to be the first to take a bath. Then at last I had a drink of sake at a drinking stand. It tasted very good. From now on, I'm having nothing more to do with *shōchū*.[†] When I went to bed I could hear someone singing a *shinnai* ballad. "The Crows of Dawn," mournful melody, enough to make the ailing traveler feel sadder than ever.

[*]The *Shushōgi* is a devotional text much used in the Sōtō school of Zen. Kannon Sutra is the popular name for chapter 25 of the Lotus Sutra, which describes the salvational power of the bodhisattva Avalokiteshvara, or Kannon.
[†]This is a recurring theme in Santōka's diaries: he drinks *shōchū*, usually because it is cheaper than sake; feels awful the next day; and vows never to drink *shōchū* again. The shōchū sold in Japan today is a much friendlier drink than that of Santōka's time.

October 30, 1930. Rain. Resting in the inn.

Raining again. Nothing to do but take a rest. Lounging around all day. I'd like to get to Nobeoka as soon as possible so I can pick up my mail at the post office, but I try to forget about that. Still, I was able to do some reading and writing, so it wasn't such a bad day. For some reason my head feels heavy, stomach and bowels no good. Probably the aftereffects of the *shōchū* I had last night, first I've had in some time. That's what's the matter, I'm sure. Makes you wonder about yourself.

> Today the whole day—not to get angry
> Today the whole day—not to tell a lie
> Today the whole day—not to waste anything

These are my Three Vows.

Not to get angry—it's possible to obey that rule, to some extent at least. Not to tell a lie—that's a hard one. It means not just not telling a lie with your mouth, but not lying in your mind or heart. You can keep from lying with your mouth—that's possible—but you have to get so you don't lie with your body either. What they call "constant practice" of the Buddhist teachings has to be like water flowing, like the blowing of the wind.

If you let yourself get angry when you're doing your begging, you'll never get anywhere. When people say no or look the other way, you have to ask what you yourself are doing wrong. In fact, I just don't have the qualifications needed to receive alms, isn't that it? . . . These days I look at the clumsy, inept frame of mind in which I go about receiving things or doing my begging, and I feel ashamed and downcast.

As far as not wasting anything goes, I observe that rule in a general way. But if you are really serious about not wasting anything, that means you have to make the best possible use of a thing, and that's extremely difficult. Take the case of sake—I like sake so I'm not going to give it up and that's that—nothing to be done about it. But drinking sake—how much merit do I acquire doing that? If I let sake get the best of me, then I'm a slave to sake, in other words, a hopeless case! . . .

And this rain coming down—whether people pray for rain or don't pray for rain, it will go on raining as long as it likes. We know that, yet we look up at the sky and hope and pray it will clear up. That's the human heart for you.

56
foul mood
soak it away
in bath water

57
passing through one day—
they let me listen
to their phonograph

58
windy town
and a Korean
whose furs don't sell

59
late at night
gamblers' voices

56 yūutsu o yu ni tokasō
57 tabi no aruhi no chikuonki kikasete morau
58 kaze no machi no kegawa urenai Senjin de
59 fukete bakuchi utsu koe

November 8, 1930. Rain. Yunoharu, Komeya, 35 sen, middling . . .

Though this is far out in the country, the hot-spring bath is still very good. The bathhouse is rather dirty, but the place is pleasantly relaxed in atmosphere and unpretentious. As soon as I arrived I took a bath, and took another when I got back from the barbershop. I'll get in the water once more before I go to bed and again tomorrow when I get up. The hot-spring water is rather sweet-and-sour tasting, not anything you could drink. But I feel it must be good for my body. Anyway, whenever I get in the bath, I can't help thinking how lucky I was to have been born in Japan. No joy in life as healthful and cheap as a bath!

I stopped at a sake brewery and found the sake very good and cheap—before I knew it, I'd had one, two, three drinks. Very tasty, though it doesn't seem to have set very well on my stomach. Tomorrow I'll have to drink lots of water.

Tonight all night I could hear the sound of water. To me it's a kind of lullaby. A bath, sake, water—these are the things that bring me a good night's sleep.

November 9, 1930. What Fayan said, "Each step is an arrival."*
Forget about past walking, don't think about future walking; one step, another step, no long ago, no now, no east or west, one step equals totality. Get this far and you understand the meaning of walking Zen.

*Fayan Wenyi (885–958) was the founder of the Chinese Fayan school of Chan, or Zen.

60
drizzly rain
only one road
to go by

61
nearly run over
by a car
cold cold road

60 shigururu ya michi wa hitosuji
61 jidōsha ni hikaren to shite samui samui michi

December 19, 1930. Haven't got a cent! . . . So, much as it irks
me, I grit my teeth and go on begging until I've got enough
for a night's lodging and a meal. When I get to an inn and
get a bath, I feel a lot better. But I hate begging. I hate wan-
dering. Most of all, I hate having to do things I hate!

December 28, 1930. Lying in bed, I think it over. I'm a fortu-
nate unfortunate, a blessed unbeliever. I can die any time, in
a serene manner, no thrashing around! I no longer need al-
cohol, no longer need calmotin,* no longer need *Geld*, no
longer need a *Frau*. . . . Well, a lie is a lie, but a feeling you
have is a feeling you have.

*Calmotin is a sedative that Santōka took frequently.

Shōwa 6 (1931)

62

cook it alone
eat it alone
New Year's soup

63
today again
no answer
rain coming on

64
red mailbox
standing
in the morning mist

65
husband-and-wife spat
over now, it seems
cold-season moon

66
a drink
would be nice now
sunset sky

62 hitori nite hitori taberu ozōni
63 kyō mo henji ga konai shigure moyō
64 asagiri no akai posuto ga tatte iru
65 fūfugenka mo itsu shika yanda kan no tsuki
66 ippai yaritai yūyake-zora

67
I make
a fire
for one

68
woman upstairs in the rain
whistles
to herself

69
cold clouds
hurrying

70
how must I look
from behind
going off in the drizzling rain?

67 hitori no hi o tsukuru (SMT)
68 ame no nikai no onna no hitori kuchibue o fuku
69 samui kumo ga isogu (SMT)
70 ushiro sugata no shigurete yuku ka (SMT)

December 28, 1931. Ah—sake, sake, sake—up to now I've lived
for sake, and this is what it's gotten me! Sake—devil or bud-
dha, poison or curative?

Shōwa 7 (1932)

January 1, 1932. What I forever aspire to is a mind calm and free from pressure, a realm of roundness, wholeness that transcends self and others. Faith is its source, haiku poems are its expression. So I have to walk, walk, walk until I get there.

January 8, 1932. Snow. Ashiya Town [no inn name] 30 sen, poor. . . . This inn too is no good. These cheap inns I stay in vary amazingly. Some of them treat you so nicely you feel like apologizing, others are as cold and unfeeling as if they were dealing with a stick or a stone. . . .

There are two Koreans staying at the inn. One older man, very Korean in appearance and manner, whom I find highly likable. I hope he manages to sell lots of writing brushes.

The other, with whom I shared lodgings, appears to be a kind of operator—of a good sort, that is. He certainly seems to know a lot about a lot of things, that is. Early in the evening we laid out our sleeping mats side by side and continued talking for some time.

January 9, 1932. . . . These days again I've been waking up every morning with a hard-on. I think of the well-known saying, "Never lend money to a man whose cock won't stand up in the morning."

January 14, 1932. . . . There's an old man on a Buddhist pilgrimage staying at the same inn, kind, polite, with something about him that reminds one of old times.

Also a young Chinese peddler, very lively, very careful with his money. I'm sure he'll manage to put away lots of it. (The Koreans are like the Japanese, always drinking and quarreling, but the Chinese never spend money foolishly. About all they do is get together sometimes and make dumplings and eat them.)

I talked with the tinker and the knife grinder until late in the evening—just idle chatter, but not bad. You never come on a tinker or a knife grinder who doesn't drink.

71
coming over the radio
song from
where I grew up

72
even in
my iron begging bowl
hailstones

73
snow's brightness
a stillness
that fills the house

74
passing through
dialects
I don't understand

71 rajio de tsunagatte kokyō no uta
72 teppatsu no naka e mo arare (SMT)
73 yuki no akarusa ga ie ippai no shizukesa (SMT)
74 wakaranai kotoba no naka o tōru

January 22, 1932. Clear. Sashi, inn called Hamaya, 25 sen, good.

This is a good inn. I seem to have gotten very good at developing a traveler's sixth sense in such matters. A wandering beggar's sixth sense.

And then, just as I was happily thinking what a nice inn it is, some strange-looking fellow comes charging in and completely destroys the mood I've been savoring. He made such a pest of himself that I finally shouted at him, and after that he more or less quieted down.

Thanks to the assistance of my old friend [Kimura] Ryokuhei, the extreme kindness of my teacher [Ogiwara] Seisensui, and generous help from other haiku friends, it appears that the first collection of Santōka's haiku will soon be coming out.* And it also seems likely that I will be able to build a small hut in the vicinity of Ryūgan-ji [in Tamana County, Kumamoto Prefecture]. Then I'll have my begging expeditions to raise money for rice, and *Sampakku* to supply money for sake.† Santōka, you're a man who lives only for haiku. Without haiku, you don't even exist!

Last night I deliberately drank too much. The glass of *shōchū* I had was particularly potent. But as a result I was able to sleep soundly. For someone always on the move like myself, lack of sleep is fatal. And alcohol works better for me than calmotin.

*Kimura Ryokuhei (1888–1968) was a doctor, haiku poet, and strong supporter of Santōka and his work. In June 1932, *Hachi no ko* (*Begging Bowl*), Santōka's first collection of haiku, was published by a small press owned by a friend.

†*Sampakku* was a poetry magazine that Santōka had begun publishing in 1931. Only three issues came out. The plan for a hut in Tamana fell through.

January 25, 1932. Clear. Sashi, the Hamaya, 25 sen, good.

The street peddler staying here says that times are really hard these days and people have gotten cleverer, so you can't make a big killing the way you used to. All the operators, big and little, say that it's gotten very hard to make any money.

In my own case, until two or three years ago I could beg at fifteen or sixteen houses and my iron begging bowl would be full of rice. Nowadays, though, I have to stop at thirty houses before I get it filled up.

Tonight I've been thinking a lot about how hard the women work in these farming and fishing villages. When I get out on the road early, I run into bunches of women, all of them middle-aged, carrying loads of vegetables, firewood, or dried fish on their backs. . . .

Sardines, sardines, sardines—all I see are sardines, all I smell are sardines, and of course all I eat are sardines!

The old Buddhist pilgrim who's staying at this inn is a phenomenal snorer. He himself admits that more than once his snoring has caused problems at the inns where he was staying. What a magnificent sound—high-pitched, low-pitched, long snores, short snores, like the roar of a monster or the thundering of the waves!

There's quite a story connected with the daughter of the inn I stayed in last night—granddaughter of the old woman who owns it. It seems she ran off with one of the guests, a Korean who goes around peddling ginseng. She had a very pretty face, but she was lame. Got to be marriageable age, but no one would have her, and she hated staying on at home. So when this Korean happened to stop at the inn, one thing led to another.

The old woman told me all about it. "You go all around the place," she said, "and you're bound to run into her somewhere. Just tell her to do her best and not worry. Tell her I'll send her some clothes and things." I told the old woman I'd be glad to do what I could, and added some prayers of my own for the young woman's happiness.

The woman who runs the inn I'm staying in tonight is a hard worker too. Nine people in the family, plus an ox. Every night four or five guests to take care of, and she has to do it all herself.

February 1, 1932. Chiwata, Nagasaki. Egawaya, 30 sen, middling.

I didn't want to stay at Takeo for long, but ended up hanging around for quite a time. I wish I could stay in Ureshino, but I can't. Things assuredly don't go the way you'd like them to!

75
ox straining
under a heavy load
its bell goes tinkle-tinkle

75 ushi wa omoni o owasarete suzu wa rin-rin

This poem expresses the way I feel about the oxen in this area. I hear the bell go tinkle-tinkle and feel happy. Then I see the load the ox is carrying and feel sad.

I can't get over the feeling that I'm bit by bit wearing out my vitality. Do I think this because I'm getting old? Because of the sake? Because of loneliness? Because of begging? Anyway, I wish I had my own bed somewhere. I want a good long rest!

I bought some fresh sardines, got someone to fix them for me, and had them with something to drink. Delicious—almost too delicious.

Don't recall what came before or after, slept the sleep that goes beyond past, present, or future.

76
came out with a voice
just like my father's—
trips are sad

77
how much longer
on the road?
clipping my nails

78
edge of town
all graveyard
and the sound of waves

79
on the road
a tooth
about to come loose

80
came along
a mountain path
talking to myself

76 chichi ni yō nita koe ga dete kuru tabi wa kanashii
77 itsu made tabi suru koto no tsume o kiru (SMT)
78 machi-hazure wa bochi to naru namioto
79 nukesō na ha o motte tabi ni oru
80 yamaji kite hitorigoto iute ita

February 28, 1932. Dark, cloudy, snow, wind. Town of Kashima. Maruya, 30 sen, middling.

Stormy every day; begging in the snow again today. Perhaps it's too much to say that the roads here are the worst in Japan, but they're rather spectacularly muddy. Shop doors plastered in mud, passersby plastered in mud. The rubber soles of my workman's *tabi* sink down in the mud and make the going very hard. At the same time, this area is unusual for the large number of sake breweries, so sake is quite cheap. Just the place for someone like me!

March 5, 1932. The woman who runs this inn is a fearful nagger. She has all the faults women are said to have, but in extra large measure. I have great respect for the husband who is patient enough to put up with such a woman. The wife in the couple in pilgrim costume seems quite ordinary in appearance and temperament, but evidently has a tendency toward hysteria in certain circumstances. I suppose it's to be expected, but one sees or hears the two of them quarreling from morning on. Rather than blaming her, I'm struck with what miserable lives people live.

The children interest me too. [When I'm begging,] some of them will say, "Nothing today, nothing today!" [as they've been told to do,] but then keep on walking along beside me. Others come up to me with a tiny handful of rice gripped in their fist—very cute. Sometimes I get mad at them, sometimes they make me feel happy—I'm a child too, I guess.

March 6, 1932. . . . The young tramp staying at this inn is a perfect example of a certain type. Doesn't drink, doesn't smoke, has no truck with women, doesn't gamble, doesn't get in fights. He just doesn't want to work. Indolence—or, to put it in extreme terms, a complete lack of any will to make a living—is surely one element in the makeup of the true tramp, a condition that seals his fate.

My Motto:

> don't get angry
> don't chatter
> don't be greedy
> walk slowly, walk steadily

81
home
a long way off
budding trees

82
I was given it
it was enough
I lay down my lone chopsticks

83
plop!
the tooth
just fell out

81 furusato wa tōku shite ki-no-me (SMT)
82 itadaite tarite hitori no hashi o oku (SMT)
83 horori to nuketa ha de wa aru (SMT)

84
through the windy tunnel
then start right in
begging

85
paint all
worn off him
Hotei still laughing*

*Hotei (Chinese, Budai) is the jolly, fat-bellied figure
known in English as the Laughing Buddha. Statues of
him are found in many temples, where visitors rub
them for good luck.

84 kaze no tonneru nukete sugu koihajimeru
85 sukkari hagete Hotei wa waraitsuzukete iru

March 27, 1932. Cloudy. Laid up all day. Finally had to take to
my bed. The fact is, the *shōchū* I drank night before last was
no good. And then the bean curd I ate yesterday seems to
have disagreed with me. Bothered by stomach pains all night,
today nothing to eat, just drinking water and staying in bed.
By evening I started getting better little by little.

Because I was in such good health, I forgot all about health.
Illness brings reflection and abstinence. Getting sick on a jour-
ney alone should be looked on as a kind of punishment.

Get sick and invariably you think about dying. I know it
would be a mess if I died like this, in a place like this. I'd only
be a trouble to myself and others.

Death! Something cold silently enveloping your whole
body, a lonely, frightening, indescribable coldness.

So today even *I* managed to keep from drinking anything (that is, drank no alcohol, only water). Didn't feel like drinking anything, knew I couldn't.

Just wish I could settle down soon in Ureshino Hot Spring. Then live out the rest of my life with the fewest possible wants in the most modest circumstances possible.

March 28, 1932. . . . Slept until close to noon. Then, since a beggar monk who doesn't beg is guilty of delinquency of a sort, I spent three hours going around the streets of the town begging. Got enough to cover daily expenses for today, though I certainly don't deserve it. A young man in his prime working steadily from morning to evening earns no more than around 80 sen a day (for a day laborer)—I can only express my thanks for the compassionate aid of the Buddha and the generosity of the public! (Actually, it's all thanks to the Buddhist robes I'm wearing.)

April 5, 1932. . . . Two people staying at this inn besides myself. A man, Korean, who peddles candy. (Very kind, even gave me a handful of his candy.) A woman with him, homely, middle-aged, a real treasure. I hear them in bed in the next room in the middle of the day, carrying on merrily. Spring has come to them too, they're in love. Blessings on them!

Had to go to the toilet a number of times again tonight—I'm walking around with a case of intestinal cramps. If I stopped eating and laid off the sake for two or three days, drank only water and stayed in bed, I could get well—but I'm afraid that's wholly beyond me.

86
tree reflections
cloud reflections
a dead cat came floating by

87
warm again tomorrow
stars out
promise of good walking

88
somewhere
inside my head
a crow is cawing

89
serenely
the puddle reflects
the figure of the child

90
went thump!
on my hat
a camellia

86 ki-kage kumo-kage neko no shigai ga nagarete kita
87 asu mo atatakō arukaseru hoshi ga dete iru
88 doko ka de atama no naka de karasu ga naku
89 mizutamari ga hogaraka ni kodomo no kage utsusu
90 kasa e pottori tsubaki datta (SMT)

April 6, 1932. What's important in life is getting the taste of things. Living, you might say, is tasting. People are happiest when they can really learn to be who they are. A beggar has to learn to be an all-out beggar. Unless he can be that, he will never taste the happiness of being a beggar. A person has no other way to live than to be out-and-out the person he is.

April 7, 1932. In Kusuku. This is a very noisy inn; lots of children, and the people seem quite poor. Rooms for guests are on the second floor, but there are no ceilings in the rooms and no *shoji*, just two or three pads of thin, hard bedding. With the whole underside of the roof open to view like this, one has a feeling not so much of the loneliness of travel as of the near misery of human life.

This inn is really depressing—the building, the bedding, the food, everything about it. But as a result, I got to spend a quiet, peaceful day and night. There are no other guests (and the lamp at least is bright), don't have to worry about the family, upstairs with one room all to myself, free to sleep or get up as I please. I seldom get to stay in an inn like this— in a good sense and in a bad sense.

I've been listening a lot to the rain—or rather, contemplating the rain. Feels more like autumn rain than spring rain. Slosh-slosh it comes droning down, and yet there's something undeniably gentle and welcome about it. Somewhere the cherries are about to burst into bloom, though I wish it weren't so chilly!

April 8, 1932. . . . This inn is spotlessly clean (and for that reason seems to attract few guests), an utter contrast to the place I stayed last night. . . .

I realize now why this inn is so unpopular. All the drifters and wheeler-dealers who stay at these cheap inns are tired of struggling to make a living and starved for some place with a homey atmosphere. For them, an inn is a home. So the most important requirement for an inn is that it be relaxed and friendly; in other words, a place where they can feel "at home." Cleanliness is very much a consideration of second or third importance. But the woman who runs this inn is overly zealous, fastidious to a fault in matters of cleanliness, and not at all accommodating.

91
new leaves on persimmon trees
flopping down
where I can see them

92
(On a visit to his hometown)
I sit down
in the midst of
my local dialect

91 kaki no wakaba ga mieru tokoro de nekorobu
92 furusato no kotoba no naka ni suwaru

93
old home
when tangerine blossoms
make a good smell

94
run-down inn
its pomegranate tree
loaded with blossoms

95
face to face
jabbering away
shelling beans

96
a snake angled
coolly
across the morning stream

97
all day
in the mountains
ants too are walking

93 furusato wa mikan no hana no niou toki
94 yasuyado no zakuro takusan hana tsuketa
95 mukiatte oshaberi no mame o muku
96 suzushiku hebi asa no nagare o yokogitta
97 yama no ichinichi ari mo aruite iru

April 12, 1932. Rain. Stayed in the inn all day resting up, a whole day and night taking things easy. . . . Spent all day putting the drafts of my poems in order. I don't feel confident enough to try to make a selection of my own work, but must get some sort of poetry collection into print. If I don't, I'll never be able to afford a place of my own to live in.

April 17, 1932. Sunny, cherry-viewing weather. . . . I deliberately went to Nakasu, where the fanciest stores in the city of Fukuoka are located, to do my begging. I did my part in the proper manner, but the results were about as I had expected—two hours of begging that brought in no more than 15 sen. I guess I got a response from about one out of every one hundred stores. I got used to receiving nothing, and when I was given something, it came rather as a big surprise. . . .

A handful of wheat—that had me feeling good again! Today at one of the places where I was begging, a child, mistaking wheat for rice, came with a handful of wheat to put in my begging bowl. I couldn't very well accept it, yet I couldn't very well *not* accept it either. (Once in Sasebo when a child came with something like that, I said, "No thank you, though I thank you all the same," whereupon the child burst into tears.) So I spread out my handkerchief and accepted the wheat in it. Then I took it back to the inn and gave it to the chickens there, but they refused to eat it. Chickens at these cheap inns are certainly fussy!

April 20, 1932. Stop to think about it, I'm not qualified to receive alms. Only those of the level of arhat or above are entitled to. So it's only natural that I meet with refusal. If I do my begging with this much understanding and resignation, then begging will become a kind of religious practice. . . .

Ground continually trampled on gets hard; people get to be somebody by being buffeted and banged around.

May 1, 1932. I seem to have a fever and I'm bothered by an aching tooth, but I do my laundry, read, write, take a walk, chat with people. . . . I'm reading the collected letters of [Ozaki] Hōsai.* Old Hōsai ignored the question of life and death—(I wouldn't go so far as to say he transcended it; on the contrary, he was in too much of a hurry to die)—and I envy him for it. Two or three times I've contemplated suicide, but even at such times I couldn't say I didn't have any attachment to life—one proof of which is the fact that I never actually did anything.

May 21, 1932. Awano [Yamaguchi Prefecture]. Today my voice projected very nicely. Not in resounding, clarion tones, perhaps, but still a voice that is distinctively my own, and about as much as I can muster, it seems. . . .

This area and this inn aren't bad. Yesterday I had three drinks of sake, so today I intended to have nothing at all to drink. But it seems I can't get along without one drink at least.

Listening as a traveler to the dialect spoken here in my home district, before I know it I'm drawn in and I too am speaking the local lingo.

*See pp. 7–8.

98
monk's robe   traveling garb
till it dries
weed bank breezes*

*Santōka had no change of clothing, so when he
washed his robe in a stream he had to wait until it
dried before he could go on.

99
raining
in my home town
walking barefoot

100
down the weedy path
I remember
to the graves

101
Flypaper
no outs—
yell in a loud voice
till you're dead

98 tabi no hōe ga kawaku made zassō no kaze
99 ame furu furusato wa hadashi de aruku (SMT)
100 omoide no kusa no komichi o ohaka made
101 ōkina koe de shinuru hoka nai

June 16, 1932. Same inn in Kawatana, [northern Kyushu]. From an unexpected quarter, a little money has come my way. I've bought some sake, gotten my head shaved, fixed myself some sliced cucumbers with vinegar—plenty to keep me busy and happy. . . . I've written replies to the correspondence that has piled up over the past several days, much to my satisfaction— ten postcards and two letters.

For the first time in five days, I had a drink of sake. It didn't taste very good, which makes me feel happy, and also rather depressed. Anyway, there's no doubt that clearing up the problem of sake is the first step in clearing up the problem of myself.

June 23, 1932. Kawatana. I didn't used to look back, but now somehow I've gotten so I do. My past is nothing but a pile of mistakes—consequently, an unending succession of regrets. Same mistakes, same regrets, repeated over and over again, right?

Too much to say I've paid what had to be paid, but I've paid as much as I could. And that makes me feel a bit brighter.

July 20, 1932. People view all things, all events in terms of what they value in life, with that as their standard. I look at everything through the eyes of sake. Gazing far off at a mountain, I think how I'd like a little drink; I see some nice vegetables and think how well they'd go with the sake. If I had such-and-such sum, I could polish off a flask; if I had this much, I could buy a bottle. You may laugh, but that's just the way I am—nothing I can do about it.

August 9, 1932. Single people, whoever they are, feel their loneliness most acutely when they come home from a trip. Everything is there just the way it was when they set out. The flower in the vase has dried up, but the desk itself hasn't moved.

102
(First days in the Gochū-an)
moving in
higan lilies
at their best

103
the rice
dutiful by nature
began to boil

104
getting used to living here
tea blossoms open
then scatter

105
live alone
and the grasses
are green so green

106
sleep
where the moonlight
reaches my bedding

102 utsurikite ohiganbana no hanazakari (SMT)
103 kokoro sunao ni gohan ga fuita (SMT)
104 suminarete cha no hana no hiraite wa chiru
105 hitori sumeba aoao o shite kusa (SMT)
106 nema made tsuki o ire neru to suru (SMT)

107
one citron
I pluck
from the evening sky

108
my spinach plants
have four leaves now

109
midday
votive lamp
keeps on burning

110
all I eat
cucumbers eggplant eggplant cucumbers
the coolness!

111
dawn coming on
honing the sickle

107 yūzora kara yuzu no hitotsu o mogitoru
108 watakushi no hōrensō ga yotsuba ni natta
109 mahiru no miakashi no moetsuzukeru
110 nasu kyūri kyūri nasu bakari taberu suzushisa
111 akete kuru kama o togu (SMT)

112
now I'm alone
flies on the flypaper
start in buzzing

113
that sound
the rain?

September 19, 1932. Anniversary of [Masaoka] Shiki's death. Shiki was a great man (though I myself don't particularly care for people of his type), a revolutionary haiku poet such as we've never seen before. I sat quietly thinking about him and about haiku. In the vase in my alcove I've put some cockscombs, and dangling at a corner of the vegetable garden is a snake gourd plant.*

October 12, 1932. In a letter to a friend I wrote: "Little by little I'm settling down. These days I put more thought and effort into my vegetable garden than I do into haiku writing. I plant the seeds myself, in the soil I've worked myself, and when the sprouts come up, I thin them. That way I can have the ones I've pulled up as part of my soup. 'Getting close to the soil'—an old-fashioned expression; old, but with a deep meaning. I feel that very keenly."

*Cockscombs and snake gourd plants (*hechima*) figure prominently in some of Masaoka Shiki's most famous haiku.

October 19, 1932. Depression sneaked up on me. There are three ways to escape it—take a walk, have a drink, go to bed. Don't feel up to a walk, haven't got the money for a drink. I tried going to bed but couldn't get to sleep. So I went to the public bath, my 2-sen 5-rin "Strategy for Dispelling Gloom."* Soaked in the hot water, shaved my whiskers, and felt much better.

October 30, 1932. Nothing for me to do but go my own way. My own way—that's unconditional. Without noticing, without realizing, I've let myself get slovenly. I've gotten used to being given things and forgotten about giving. I make things easy for myself, and I despair of myself. It's all right to be poor, but not to stink of poverty.

114
mornings are good!
leaves fallen
leaves yet to fall

115
in the autumn night
somewhere
playing a samisen

114 asa wa yoi kana ochita ha mo ochinu ha mo
115 aki no yo no doko ka de shamisen hiite iru

*The rin was worth one-thousandth the value of the yen.

116
someone there
picking persimmons
in the rain

117
tea blossoms
winter coming
nearer me now

116 hito ga ite shigureru kaki o moide ita
117 cha no hana ya mi ni chikaku fuyu no kite iru

December 14, 1932. Not a smidgen of tobacco left. I dug around in the ashes of the brazier and came up with a half-smoked Golden Bat. And I was delighted—like a man panning for gold who comes on a bit of gold dust. But what shameful behavior! Shows what a disgusting beggar I am at heart, a slave to desire!

Shōwa 8 (1933)
118
the crow at New Year's
caw–caw

119
here in the hush
of snow
falling on snow

118 oshōgatsu no karasu kaa-kaa (SMT)
119 yuki e yuki furu shizukesa no oru

120
thatched roof
making me nice rows
of icicles

121
snow falling
alone in the middle of it
build a fire

122
snow falling
one by one
they go

123
even the snow
can't be good snow
factory zone smoke

120 waraya shitashiku tsurara o tsurane
121 yuki furu sono naka hitori to shite hi o moyasu
122 yuki furu hitori hitori yuku (SMT)
123 yuki mo yoi yuki ni naranai kōjō chitai no kemuri (SMT)

February 2, 1933. If there is anything good in my life—or I should say, anything good in my poems—it comes from the fact that they are not imitative, they are not contrived, they tell few lies, they're never forced.

124
after all
alone is best
weeds

125
get drunk
you hear all sorts of voices
winter rain

124 yappari hitori ga yoroshii zassō
125 yoeba iro-iro no koe ga kikoeru fuyuame

March 28, 1933. Even if it means nothing to eat, I don't want to do any more of that hateful begging! People who have never done any begging seem to have difficulty understanding how I feel about this.

126
warm day—
and still
some food on hand

127
babying it
the tooth so sensitive
to cold things

126 nukui hi no, mada taberu mono wa aru (SMT)
127 tsumetasa no ha ni shimiru ha o itawarō

128
spring rain
at dawn came a sound of water

129
there
where the fire was
something blooming

128 harusame no yoake no mizuoto ga naridashita
129 yake-ato nani yara saite iru

June 11, 1933 [returning from a begging trip to northern Kyushu].
Got back to my hut at three o'clock. Traveling by train, in
two hours I covered a distance that would have taken me
two days on foot. Once again I am profoundly impressed by
the advantages of modern civilization and the usefulness of
money.

Dead tired, I went to bed as soon as I got home. . . . Is it
because I've been drinking too much? Because of my age?
Because of the heat? Anyway, I was worn out. And some-
how, because I was sleeping in my own bed again, I was able
to go to sleep with a mind at ease.

So good to have my own hut! It's lonely but it's quiet; I'm
poor but I'm at peace.

130
Returning to My Hut
coming back after a long time
bamboo shoots
nosing up all over

131
you said you'd come tomorrow
I'm cooking up
the rain-soaked butterbur*

*Butterbur (*fuki*) is a wild plant whose stalks are edible.

132
soppy with morning dew
I go off
any direction I please

130 hisabisa modoreba takenoko nyoki-nyoki (SMT)
131 asu wa kuru to iu ame no fuki o nite oku
132 asatsuyu shittori ikitai hō e yuku (SMT)

July 6, 1933. I'm turning into a kind of haiku factory. Watch out! Careful here! One good poem is worth more than a thousand junky ones!

133
the figs
I can reach—
their ripeness

133 te ga todoku ichijiku no urezama (SMT)

134
overhead
cicadas in the pines
in front a sound of waves

135
butterflies
in the wind
seeing them on their way

136
cuckoo
tomorrow I'll cross over
that mountain

137
long day
going from house to house
nobody home

138
back road
just as before
choked with summer weeds

134 matsuzemi ga atama no ue de namioto o mae
135 kaze no chōchō no yukue o miokuru
136 hototogisu asu wa ano yama koete yukō (SMT)
137 hi ga nagai ie kara ie e rusu bakari
138 uramichi wa natsugusa ga tōrenaku shita mamma

July 13, 1933. Stretched out alone under a mosquito net, reading a book I like—this is the Pure Land, the Land of Supreme Bliss!

July 16, 1933. Up to now my haiku have been like wine—not bad wine, but not good wine either. From now on my haiku will be more like water—clear, bright, not flowing over but rippling right along—or, I hope that's what they'll be like.

July 20, 1933. Pleasant morning, but I'm upset because I broke the chimney on my kerosene lamp. The chimney was cracked anyway, so I don't mind about that, but I'm annoyed at myself for breaking it. More precisely, I hate being the kind of person who is so careless and scatterbrained that he breaks things when he has no intention of doing so. . . . The chimney was already cracked, but now that it's broken I'm in a fix. No money to buy a new chimney, I'm forced to spend the evening ruminating in the dark.*

139
nothing else
but to die
mountains misted over

140
truly good rain
falling
good for the figs too

139 shinu yori hoka nai yama ga kasunde iru
140 shinjitsu yoi ame ga furu ichijiku no mi mo

*Santōka had electricity in his cottage, but the power had been cut off because of nonpayment of bills.

141
busy pulling away
at paddy weeds—
those big balls*

*In Santōka's time, Japanese farmers working in
the fields in hot weather often wore only a simple
loincloth.

142
wearing rags
cool
one man walks along

143
frog
still a baby
middle of the green leaf

144
lunch today
sitting on the grass
two tomatoes

145
nice inn
mountains all around
sake store in front

141 sesse to tagusa toru ōki na kōgan
142 boro kite suzushii hitori ga aruku
143 kaeru osanaku aoi ha no mannaka ni
144 kyō no ohiru wa kusa ni suwatte tomato futatsu
145 yoi yado de dochira mo yama de mae wa sakaya de

146
feel of the needle
when at last
you get the thread through it

147
pick one
have it for supper*

*"One" is the fruit of an old citron tree that grew in
back of the Gochū-an. See poem 107.

148
no desire to die
no desire to live
the wind blows over me

149
feeling lonely
getting in
the hot bath water

150
hadn't noticed
moon gone down
thick darkness all around

146 yatto ito ga tōtta hari no kanshoku
147 hitotsu moide gohan ni shō
148 shinitaku mo ikitaku mo nai kaze ga furete yuku
149 sabishū nari atsui yu ni hairu
150 itsu-no-ma-ni-yara tsuki wa ochiteru yami ga shimijimi

151
seeing someone off
coming back alone
muddy road

152
autumn winds already
Lord Jizō*
only his head is new

*Lord Jizō is a Buddhist saint and protector of
children. Stone statues of him are stationed here
and there along the roads and are fitted with a new
head if the old one falls off.

153
(In sickness)
woke up suddenly
tears coming down

151 hito o miokuri hitori de kaeru nukarumi (SMT)
152 mō akikaze no Jizōsama no kubi dake atarashii
153 futo mezametara namida koborete ita

Shōwa 9 (1934)

154
rustle rustle
snow on bamboo grass

155
the leafless tree
is drying
my *tabi* socks

154 sarasara sasa no yuki
155 kareki wa tabi o kawakashite iru

February 7, 1934. Mind downcast, as though dumped in a muddy pond. I try to calm it but can't settle down. Get settled down but still I'm fretting. Physiologically a sign of alcohol addiction, psychologically a symptom of alienation and loneliness—I understand this, understand it all too well. What to do about it?

February 15, 1934. The fusing of the subjective and the objective into a single entity, or the fusion of the self and nature—I think we can distinguish two forms that this process may take, namely, that in which the individual simply undergoes fusion, melts into it, as it were; and that in which he actively seeks to achieve fusion. Or, to put it another way, there are two types of persons, those who throw themselves into the bosom of nature, and those who absorb nature into themselves. In either case, however, there is no difference in the realm achieved, a realm in which nature is one with the self; the self, one with nature.

If human beings are permitted no imaginings, no fancy, then there can be no art. The truths of art derive from the facts of daily life, but those truths are not necessarily facts themselves. The truths of the artist are what, in the artist's mind, he wishes would be, what ought to be, what cannot help but be, and these constitute the content of his creation.

156
jonquils in a jar
all the spring I need

156 tsubo ni suisen watakushi no haru wa jūbun

157
snow shining
on far-off mountains
I'll take a trip

158
no road
but this one
spring snow coming down

159
far enough
for today—
I undo my straw sandals

160
nice road
going to a nice building
crematorium

161
a crow walking there
new shoots of grass

157 tōyama no yuki no hikaru ya tabidatsu to suru
158 kono michi shika nai haru no yuki furu (SMT)
159 kyō wa koko made no waraji o nugu (SMT)
160 yoi michi ga yoi tatemono e yakiba desu (SMT)
161 karasu ga aruite iru moedashita kusa

162
tree fallen over
sitting down on it

163
face to face
bath water brimming over

164
bamboo shoot
on its way to becoming bamboo
how honest of it!

165
sheath stripped away
bamboo shoot shines
green green

162 ki ga taorete iru koshi o kakeru
163 mukiōte yu no afururu o
164 take to nariyuku take no ko no sunao naru kana
165 ao-ao to take no ko no kawa nuide hikaru

July 14, 1934. Sending off some haiku. I write a lot of haiku, but when it comes to sending any off for publication, the number is few. There just aren't that many that I have confidence in.

166
no one comes
to see me
peppers turning red

167
swallow on the wing
journey after journey
put on straw sandals

168
camellia
I turned to look back at
red

169
seeds dropped
sprouted where they fell
loquats piled on loquats

170
road running straight ahead
rolling a big thing
down on me

166 dare mo konai tōgarashi akō naru (SMT)
167 tsubame tobikau tabi kara tabi e waraji o haku (SMT)
168 furikaeru tsubaki ga akai
169 ochite sono mama mebaeta biwa ni biwa
170 michi ga massugu ōkina mono o korogashite kuru

171
somehow
I get to go on living
among summer grasses

172
(Scene in the Yuda "Thousand-Persons
Hot-Spring Bath")
cocks and cunts
hot water
full and flowing over

173
you came the back way
covered with seeds
from all those grasses

171 tomokaku mo ikasarete wa iru natsugusa no naka (SMT)
172 chimpoko mo ososo mo waite afureru yu
173 ura kara kite kurete kusa no mi darake

August 2, 1934. Sometimes a life where I want to die, some-
times a life where I can't die, sometimes close to the bud-
dhas, sometimes one with the devils. Sorry to discover the
animal in myself. Then at last the night is over, the morning
sun good. . . . Today again, must get myself in shape, make
preparations so I'm ready to die any time.

174
(Scene with an itinerant peddler)
heavy load   hot weather
dickering over price
I think he'll come down a little

175
bush clover swaying
bush clover bending
its blossoms shower down

176
in the sweet taste
of a ripe persimmon too
I remember my grandmother

177
I sit
in the beauty
of grasses as they wither

178
snake
sunning himself—
get back in your hole!

174 omokute atsukute negirarete makeru no ka
175 yurete wa hagi no fushite wa hagi no koboruru hana
176 jukushi no amasa mo obāsan no omokage
177 kare yuku kusa no utsukushisa ni suwaru
178 hebi ga hinata ni, mō ana e haire

179
didn't mean to think of it
still I thought of it
rain coming down

179 kangaeru tomo naku kangaete ita shigurete ita

November 13, 1934. Twenty years since I began writing haiku, and I realize more than ever: haiku writing is a practice that's easy to take up, but very difficult to really get anywhere in. It's like Buddhism in that respect.

November 26, 1934. Loving sake, savoring sake, enjoying sake is not so bad. But drowning in sake, rioting in sake—that won't do! Running around drinking in this messy way—utterly stupid!

180
owl in owl's way
I in mine
can't get to sleep

181
wind blows right through me
plop
and I fall over dead

180 fukurō wa fukurō de watashi wa watashi de
nemurenai (SMT)
181 kaze ga fukinukeru korori-to shinde iru

December 12, 1934. My sex drive is gone; my appetite is bit by bit disappearing. What will go next?

December 16, 1934. I'm a man who has never known love. I've never loved a woman, never been loved by a woman. . . . There were times when I thought that a woman's body was good, but somehow I could never come to like the woman herself.

182
(Date uncertain, for a neighborhood drinking
companion)
come tramping over
fallen leaves—
I know the sound of your footsteps

183
(Date uncertain)
more and more like him
my father
no longer alive

184
(Date uncertain)
all withered—
grasses I walk over
going nowhere

182 ochiba fumikuru sono ashioto wa shitte iru (SMT)
183 dandan nite kuru kuse no chichi wa mō inai
184 ate mo naku fumiaruku kusa wa mina karetari

Shōwa 10 (1935)

185
suddenly
that hungover face
bucket water

185 futo yoizame no kao go aru baketsu no mizu

Oak leaves so easily alarmed. The slightest breeze and they
make a racket. But even after they're dead they don't fall off
the branches. Day and night the leaves chatter back and
forth. When I come home late at night the oak leaves greet
me, rattling overhead. No one coming to visit, nowhere to
go, and they just hang up there. The dried-up leaves, flut-
tering, one leaf, two leaves—these are the leaves of the oak.*

186
oak leaves
all blown down
in the spring wind

187
boiled bean curd
eating it alone
it wobbles

186 harukaze no nara no ha no sukkari ochita
187 hitori taberu yudōfu ugoku

*Prose piece, ZS, vol. 6, p. 426.

188
loquats
so beautiful
but she doesn't smile

189
hangover
and blossoms
scattering scattering

190
camellia blossoms falling
look up and see
others still in bloom

188 biwa no utsukushisa kanojo wa warawanai
189 yoizame no hana koboreru koboreru
190 tsubaki ochite iru aogeba saite iru

June 24, 1935. Get rid of attachment—attachment to sake, to poetry writing, to you yourself!

191
no regrets
evening
taro leaves flap-flapping

191 omoioku koto wa nai yūbe imo no ha hirahira

192
something about the water
even cloud reflections
can't settle down

193
finish the last
of the sake
hear the wind

194
narrow path
deep into green leaves
a grave

195
footsteps approaching
now they've gone away
fallen leaves

192 mizu no kumo kage mo ochitsukasenai mono ga aru (SMT)
193 aru dake no sake o tabe kaze o kiki
194 aoba no oku e nao komichi ga atte haka
195 ashioto ga kite sono mama shimatta ochiba

Shōwa 11 (1936)

196
spring snow falling
woman
so very beautiful

197
got this far
drink some water
and go on

198
(Osaka, Dōtombori entertainment district)
everyone
with a house to go home to
evening crowds

199
later on
a cool moon comes up
between the buildings

200
(At Eihei-ji, head temple of the Sōtō Zen school)
butterfly
fluttering fluttering
up over the temple roof finial

196 haru no yuki furu onna wa makoto utsukushiii (SMT)
197 koko made koshi o mizu nonde saru
198 minna kaeru ie wa aru yūbe no yukiki (SMT)
199 fukeru to suzushii tsuki ga biru no aida kara (SMT)
200 chōchō hirahira iraka o koeta (SMT)

201
(At Eihei-ji)
over the mountain's silence
silent rain

202
crossing water
to no one in particular
good-bye!

201 yama no shizukesa e shizuka naru ame
202 mizu o wataru dare ni tomo naku sayōnara

August 17, 1936. I can't stand to be alone unless I have a drink. Then if I have a drink, I go out somewhere, and if I go out, nothing good comes of it! Can't I ever learn to settle down quietly by myself? What a sorry case I am!

October 10, 1936. To do *takuhatsu* and then not devote yourself to religious practice as a disciple of the Buddha should is to solicit aid by fraudulent means. To go on begging expeditions and then squander the resources you receive—this too is a species of fraud. If you claim to be a Buddhist but fail to devote all your energies to the way of the Buddha, what is this but to engage in malpractice?

203
tree leaves shining
all autumn clouds now

204
the mail came
and after that
just persimmon leaves falling

203 ko no ha hikaru kumo ga aki ni narikitta
204 yūbin ga kite sore kara kaki no ha no chiru dake

October 12, 1936. Persimmon leaves—I wonder if that wouldn't be a good title for my next haiku collection. Not the fruit of the persimmon, not the persimmon tree—the leaves of the persimmon.*

December 8, 1936. Haiku-like haiku aren't particularly bad. But haiku that don't seem haiku-like at all—nowadays that's the kind I'm after.

*Santōka did in fact use this as the title of one of his haiku collections included in *Sōmokutō* (*Grass and Tree Stupa* [SMT]). Poem 204 is also included there, though in a slightly revised, and in my opinion a somewhat less effective, form.

Shōwa 12 (1937)

205
taking a leisurely piss
new grasses shoot up all over

206
today's delight
mountain after mountain
the color of budding trees

205 nombiri shito suru kusa no me darake (SMT)
206 kyō no yorokobi wa yama mata yama no mebuku iro

January 26, 1937. For breakfast, noodles; for lunch, nothing; for
supper, *daikon* radish—because that's all there is. . . . Today
again, waiting for a letter from [my son] K. . . . In the
evening, the fact that there's no kerosene for the lamp led to
the composing of a number of haiku—didn't get to sleep
until close on dawn. A beautiful moon—couldn't help being
profoundly moved.

January 27, 1937. At last a letter from K, much to my relief. Went out immediately, paid off what bills I could, bought what I could. Today's purchases (rather a lot):

postcards—45 sen
sake—60 sen
charcoal—1 yen 20 sen
Nadeshiko (tobacco)—32 sen
candles—6 sen
rice—62 sen
noodles—10 sen
sardines—6 sen
bean paste—9 sen
dried anchovies—15 sen

207
green—
drunk and it gets
even greener

208
katydid katydid
nothing to do
but cry

207 midori yoeba iyo-iyo midori
208 gachagacha gachagacha naku yori hoka nai

Shōwa 13 (1938)

209
open the window
a whole windowful
of spring

210
Heaven
doesn't kill me
it makes me write poems

211
(Santōka offers a dish of noodles before the
memorial tablet of his mother on the anniversary
of her death, March 6)
an offering
of noodles
I'm having some too

212
alone
crossing the mountain—
another mountain

209 mado akete mado ippai no haru
210 ten ware of korosazu shite shi o tsukurashimu
211 udon sonaete, watakushi mo itadakimasu
212 hitori yama koete mata yama

July 11, 1938. Today is the day the ashes of the dead soldiers arrive. I caught the 10 o'clock bus to Yamaguchi. . . . At Yamaguchi Station, a guard of honor, families of the deceased, onlookers standing around under the glaring summer sky, waiting, myself among them. Hot, hot! Now and then, spatters of rain, like tears from the sky.

A little past twelve the train arrived. Ah—two hundred and thirty or forty some dead, a "triumphal return" with no hurrahs, a pitiful scene. Alongside the white boxes, two or three memorial bunches of bellflowers, two or three pigeons appearing, circling in the sky above. Sounds of muffled weeping, muted volley of rifles, sad notes of bugles, as the procession moves solemnly through the crowd, taking the dead men back to their home unit.

213
("Home Front")
valiantly—that too
pitifully—that too
white boxes

214
("Home Front")
drops of sweat
plop-plopping
on blank white boxes

213 isamashiku mo kanashiku mo shiroi hako (SMT)
214 poroporo shitataru ase ga mashiro no hako ni (SMT)

215
("Home Front")
town festival
as bones
coming home for it?

216
("Home Front")
scarecrow too
bravely waving
the Rising Sun flag

217
once out of town
a moon
and a long bridge

218
in the wind
walking alone
blaming myself

219
nothing left of the house
I was born in
fireflies

215 machi ni omatsuri okotsu to natte kaerareta ka (SMT)
216 kakashi mo gatchiri Hinomaru futte iru (SMT)
217 machi o nukeru to tsuki ga aru nagai hashi ga aru
218 kaze no naka onore o semetsutsu aruku
219 umareta ie wa atokata mo nai hōtaru (SMT)

220
belly button
it gathers up
all the sweat

220 heso ga ase tamete iru (*SMT*)

September 25, 1938. Today I managed to write ten haiku. To be sure, they're about as much good as bits of broken tile. Still, if I polish them up, they'll probably shine insofar as bits of tile can. So it's polish, polish! Polish until they shine!

221
late-fall drizzle
last of the rice
cooked up nicely

Shōwa 14 (1939)
222
from the spring mountain
loose stones
clattering down

223
sparrows chattering
can't pay back
what I borrowed

221 shigururu ya arudake no gohan yō taketa (*SMT*)
222 haru no yama kara korokoro ishikoro
223 suzume no oshaberi karita mono ga kaesenai

224
Elevator Girl
going up going down
saying the same words over and over
the long long day

225
all through my body
goodness of mountains
good taste of water

226
the mountain's stillness
white blossoms

227
Nara Park
pagoda
five stories high
the slow-moving deer

228
Sleeping in the Field
doze off
dream of home
reed leaves rustling

224 agattari sagattari onaji kotoba kurikaeshite nagai nagai hi
225 yama no yosa o mizu no umasa o karada ippai
226 yama no shizukesa wa shiroi hana (SMT)
227 tō wa gojū yūyū to shite shika
228 madoromeba furusato no yume ashi hazure

229
red of dawn sky
red of sunset sky
nothing to eat

230
willow leaves scatter
rushing off on a trip
going nowhere

231
this trip
likely the one I'll die on
dandelions gone to fuzz

232
nowhere to put up
the dark came on
suddenly

233
bright moonlight tonight
here's a boat
I'll sleep in it

229 asa-yake yū-yake taberu mono ga nai (SMT)
230 yanagi chiru isoide ate mo nai tabi e
231 kono tabi shi no tabi de arō hohoke tampopo
232 tomaru tokoro ga nai dokari to kureta
233 tsukiyo akarui fune ga atte sono naka de neru

November 4, 1939 [on a walking trip in Shikoku]. The rain began coming down in earnest, and the wind was blowing hard. . . . It blew my hat off, and my glasses went flying too—what a mess! But a grade-school student passing by retrieved them for me—many many thanks! Rain kept getting worse, wind blowing stronger all the time—nothing to do but stop for the night at Okutomo—but none of the inns would have me. Let it be! is all I say and, looking like a drowned rat, I walk on. Finally can't go on any longer and take shelter in the lee of a roadside warehouse. I wring out my clothes, eat lunch, stay there for two hours. Deluge!—no other word for it—violent wind lashing it around, sheets of rain streaming sideways like a loose blind. I felt as though I'd been bashed flat by Heaven—a rather splendid feeling in fact. With evening I was able to make it as far as Shishikui, but again nobody would take me in. Finally got to Kannoura, where I found an inn that would give me lodging, much to my relief.

234
nothing else to do
spread fallen leaves   sleep on them
the mountain's beauty

235
soaking deeper and deeper
into the rocks
fall night rain

234 ochiba shiite neru yori hoka nai yama no utsukushisa
235 ishi ni shikushiku shimitōru aki no yo no ame nari

236
autumn wind
for all my walking—
for all my walking—

237
long night
barked at by a dog
the whole night through

238
goat bleating
pulling the goat
a woman comes this way

Shōwa 15 (1940)
239
sake slopping over
on our knees
wish we were together

240
morning bath
hot water full and spilling over
me in the middle of it

236 aki kaze aruite mo aruite mo
237 yo no nagasa yodōshi inu ni hoerarete
238 yagi naite yagi o hippatte kuru onna
239 hiza ni sake no koboruru ni aitō naru
240 asayu konkon afururu mannaka no watakushi

March 28, 1940. I've been seeing too much of other people, and that's not good. A human being is one among other human beings, but sometimes it's good to be a human being apart from others, to look around at yourself. Recently I've been having too much to do with others. Think it over!

241
facing this way
opening
white flowers smell good

242
water   dragonflies
me too
all of us flow along

241 kochira muite hiraite shiroi hana niou
242 mizu ga tombo ga watashi mo nagare yuku

August 28, 1940. The early morning was so chilly that I had to put on a bathrobe. I have no money to buy new clogs, so I don't go outdoors.* I've mended an old torn pair of straw house slippers; for the time being, I needn't go completely barefoot.

In the evening I crawled under the mosquito net and read by the uncertain light of the lamp. . . . A cockroach came racing around inside the mosquito net. I smacked and killed him, but afterward kept feeling bad about what I'd done. Hey, old cockroach, where did you sneak in from? There are none of your buddies in here, are there?

Sake is my koan. If I could understand sake—if I could learn the true way to enjoy sake, it would be my awakening, my breakthrough!

---

*The day before, Santōka had broken his only pair of *geta* (wooden clogs).

243
waiting for what?
each day   each day
more fallen leaves pile up

244
fall rain coming down
persimmon leaves
more beautiful than ever

245
Otata will come again
one day
late fall in the mountains*

*Otata was a woman who went around selling fish
in the area of Santōka's cottage in Matsuyama.

243 nani o matsu hi ni hi ni ochiba fukō naru (SMT)
244 shigurete kaki no ha no iyo-iyo utsukushiku
245 Otata mo aru hi wa kite kureru yama no aki fukaku

October 6, 1940. Late in the season as it is, a dragonfly has ap-
peared and is flying around me. Keep on flying as long as you
can—your flying days will soon be over.*

*This is the last entry in Santōka's diary, written four days be-
fore his death.

Bibliography of Works in English

Abrams, James. "Hail in the Begging Bowl: The Odyssey and Po-
etry of Santōka." *Monumenta Nipponica* 32 (1997): 269–302.

Keene, Donald. *Dawn to the West: Japanese Literature of the Modern
Era.* Vol. 2. New York: Holt, Rinehart and Winston, 1984.

Santōka Taneda. *Santoka: Grass and Tree Cairn.* Translated by Hi-
roaki Sato. Winchester, Va.: Red Moon Press, 2002.

Stevens, John. *Mountain Tasting: Zen Haiku by Santōka Taneda.* New
York: Weatherhill, 1980.

Ueda, Makoto. *Modern Japanese Poets and the Nature of Literature.*
Stanford, Calif.: Stanford University Press, 1983. [Especially on
Ogiwara Seisensui, pp. 284–334]

Other Works in the Columbia Asian Studies Series

Translations from the Asian Classics

Major Plays of Chikamatsu, tr. Donald Keene 1961

Four Major Plays of Chikamatsu, tr. Donald Keene. Paperback ed. only. 1961; rev. ed. 1997

Records of the Grand Historian of China, translated from the Shih chi of Ssu-ma Ch'ien, tr. Burton Watson, 2 vols. 1961

Instructions for Practical Living and Other Neo-Confucian Writings by Wang Yang-ming, tr. Wing-tsit Chan 1963

Hsün Tzu: Basic Writings, tr. Burton Watson, paperback ed. only. 1963; rev. ed. 1996

Chuang Tzu: Basic Writings, tr. Burton Watson, paperback ed. only. 1964; rev. ed. 1996

The Mahābhārata, tr. Chakravarthi V. Narasimhan. Also in paperback ed. 1965; rev. ed. 1997

The Manyōshū, Nippon Gakujutsu Shinkōkai edition 1965

Su Tung-p'o: Selections from a Sung Dynasty Poet, tr. Burton Watson. Also in paperback ed. 1965

Bhartrihari: Poems, tr. Barbara Stoler Miller. Also in paperback ed. 1967

Basic Writings of Mo Tzu, Hsün Tzu, and Han Fei Tzu, tr. Burton Watson. Also in separate paperback eds. 1967

The Awakening of Faith, Attributed to Aśvaghosha, tr. Yoshito S. Hakeda. Also in paperback ed. 1967

Reflections on Things at Hand: The Neo-Confucian Anthology, comp. Chu Hsi and Lü Tsu-ch'ien, tr. Wing-tsit Chan 1967

The Platform Sutra of the Sixth Patriarch, tr. Philip B. Yampolsky. Also in paperback ed. 1967

Essays in Idleness: The Tsurezuregusa of Kenkō, tr. Donald Keene. Also in paperback ed. 1967

The Pillow Book of Sei Shōnagon, tr. Ivan Morris, 2 vols. 1967

Two Plays of Ancient India: The Little Clay Cart and the Minister's Seal, tr. J. A. B. van Buitenen 1968

The Complete Works of Chuang Tzu, tr. Burton Watson 1968

The Romance of the Western Chamber (Hsi Hsiang chi), tr. S. I. Hsiung. Also in paperback ed. 1968

The Manyōshū, Nippon Gakujutsu Shinkōkai edition. Paperback ed. only. 1969

Records of the Historian: Chapters from the Shih chi of Ssu-ma Ch'ien, tr. Burton Watson. Paperback ed. only. 1969

Cold Mountain: 100 Poems by the T'ang Poet Han-shan, tr. Burton Watson. Also in paperback ed. 1970

Twenty Plays of the Nō Theatre, ed. Donald Keene. Also in paperback ed. 1970

Chūshingura: The Treasury of Loyal Retainers, tr. Donald Keene. Also in paperback ed. 1971; rev. ed. 1997

The Zen Master Hakuin: Selected Writings, tr. Philip B. Yampolsky 1971

Chinese Rhyme-Prose: Poems in the Fu Form from the Han and Six Dynasties Periods, tr. Burton Watson. Also in paperback ed. 1971

Kūkai: Major Works, tr. Yoshito S. Hakeda. Also in paperback ed. 1972

The Old Man Who Does as He Pleases: Selections from the Poetry and Prose of Lu Yu, tr. Burton Watson 1973

The Lion's Roar of Queen Śrīmālā, tr. Alex and Hideko Wayman 1974

Courtier and Commoner in Ancient China: Selections from the History of the Former Han by Pan Ku, tr. Burton Watson. Also in paperback ed. 1974

Japanese Literature in Chinese, vol. 1: *Poetry and Prose in Chinese by Japanese Writers of the Early Period*, tr. Burton Watson 1975

Japanese Literature in Chinese, vol. 2: *Poetry and Prose in Chinese by Japanese Writers of the Later Period*, tr. Burton Watson 1976

Scripture of the Lotus Blossom of the Fine Dharma, tr. Leon Hurvitz. Also in paperback ed. 1976

Love Song of the Dark Lord: Jayadeva's Gītagovinda, tr. Barbara Stoler Miller. Also in paperback ed. Cloth ed. includes critical text of the Sanskrit. 1977; rev. ed. 1997

Ryōkan: Zen Monk-Poet of Japan, tr. Burton Watson 1977

Calming the Mind and Discerning the Real: From the Lam rim chen mo of Tsoṇ-kha-pa, tr. Alex Wayman 1978

The Hermit and the Love-Thief: Sanskrit Poems of Bhartrihari and Bilhaṇa, tr. Barbara Stoler Miller 1978

The Lute: Kao Ming's P'i-p'a chi, tr. Jean Mulligan. Also in paperback ed. 1980

A Chronicle of Gods and Sovereigns: Jinnō Shōtōki of Kitabatake Chikafusa, tr. H. Paul Varley 1980

Among the Flowers: The Hua-chien chi, tr. Lois Fusek 1982

Grass Hill: Poems and Prose by the Japanese Monk Gensei, tr. Burton Watson 1983

Doctors, Diviners, and Magicians of Ancient China: Biographies of Fangshih, tr. Kenneth J. DeWoskin. Also in paperback ed. 1983

Theater of Memory: The Plays of Kālidāsa, ed. Barbara Stoler Miller. Also in paperback ed. 1984

The Columbia Book of Chinese Poetry: From Early Times to the Thirteenth Century, ed. and tr. Burton Watson. Also in paperback ed. 1984

Poems of Love and War: From the Eight Anthologies and the Ten Long Poems of Classical Tamil, tr. A. K. Ramanujan. Also in paperback ed. 1985

The Bhagavad Gita: Krishna's Counsel in Time of War, tr. Barbara Stoler Miller 1986

The Columbia Book of Later Chinese Poetry, ed. and tr. Jonathan Chaves. Also in paperback ed. 1986

The Tso Chuan: Selections from China's Oldest Narrative History, tr. Burton Watson 1989

Waiting for the Wind: Thirty-six Poets of Japan's Late Medieval Age, tr. Steven Carter 1989

Selected Writings of Nichiren, ed. Philip B. Yampolsky 1990

Saigyō, Poems of a Mountain Home, tr. Burton Watson 1990

The Book of Lieh Tzu: A Classic of the Tao, tr. A. C. Graham. Morningside ed. 1990

The Tale of an Anklet: An Epic of South India—The Cilappatikāram of Iḷaṇkō Aṭikaḷ, tr. R. Parthasarathy 1993

Waiting for the Dawn: A Plan for the Prince, tr. and introduction by Wm. Theodore de Bary 1993

Yoshitsune and the Thousand Cherry Trees: A Masterpiece of the Eigh-teenth-Century Japanese Puppet Theater, tr., annotated, and with introduction by Stanleigh H. Jones, Jr. 1993

The Lotus Sutra, tr. Burton Watson. Also in paperback ed. 1993

The Classic of Changes: A New Translation of the I Ching as Interpreted by Wang Bi, tr. Richard John Lynn 1994

Beyond Spring: Tz'u Poems of the Sung Dynasty, tr. Julie Landau 1994

The Columbia Anthology of Traditional Chinese Literature, ed. Victor H. Mair 1994

Scenes for Mandarins: The Elite Theater of the Ming, tr. Cyril Birch 1995

Letters of Nichiren, ed. Philip B. Yampolsky; tr. Burton Watson et al. 1996

Unforgotten Dreams: Poems by the Zen Monk Shōtetsu, tr. Steven D. Carter 1997

The Vimalakirti Sutra, tr. Burton Watson 1997

Japanese and Chinese Poems to Sing: The Wakan rōei shū, tr. J. Thomas Rimer and Jonathan Chaves 1997

Breeze Through Bamboo: Kanshi of Ema Saikō, tr. Hiroaki Sato 1998

A Tower for the Summer Heat, Li Yu, tr. Patrick Hanan 1998

Traditional Japanese Theater: An Anthology of Plays, Karen Brazell 1998

The Original Analects: Sayings of Confucius and His Successors (0479–0249), E. Bruce Brooks and A. Taeko Brooks 1998

The Classic of the Way and Virtue: A New Translation of the Tao-te ching *of Laozi as Interpreted by Wang Bi,* tr. Richard John Lynn 1999

The Four Hundred Songs of War and Wisdom: An Anthology of Poems from Classical Tamil, The Puranāṉūṟu, ed. and trans. George L. Hart and Hank Heifetz 1999

Original Tao: Inward Training (Nei-yeh) *and the Foundations of Taoist Mysticism,* by Harold D. Roth 1999

Lao Tzu's Tao Te Ching: A Translation of the Startling New Documents Found at Guodian, Robert G. Henricks 2000

The Shorter Columbia Anthology of Traditional Chinese Literature, ed. Victor H. Mair 2000

Mistress and Maid (Jiaohongji) by Meng Chengshun, tr. Cyril Birch 2001

Chikamatsu: Five Late Plays, tr. and ed. C. Andrew Gerstle 2001

The Essential Lotus: Selections from the Lotus Sutra, tr. Burton Watson 2002

Early Modern Japanese Literature: An Anthology, 1600–1900, ed. Haruo Shirane 2002

The Sound of the Kiss, or The Story That Must Never Be Told: Pingali Suranna's Kalapurnodayamu, tr. Vecheru Narayana Rao and David Shulman 2003

The Selected Poems of Du Fu, tr. Burton Watson 2003

Far Beyond the Field: Haiku by Japanese Women, tr. Makoto Ueda 2003

Just Living: Poems and Prose by the Japanese Monk Tonna, ed. and tr. Steven D. Carter 2003

Han Feizi: Basic Writings, tr. Burton Watson 2003

Mozi: Basic Writings, tr. Burton Watson 2003

Xunzi: Basic Writings, tr. Burton Watson 2003

Zhuangzhi: Basic Writings, tr. Burton Watson 2003

Modern Asian Literature

Modern Japanese Drama: An Anthology, ed. and tr. Ted. Takaya. Also in paperback ed. 1979

Mask and Sword: Two Plays for the Contemporary Japanese Theater, by Yamazaki Masakazu, tr. J. Thomas Rimer 1980

Yokomitsu Riichi, Modernist, Dennis Keene 1980

Nepali Visions, Nepali Dreams: The Poetry of Laxmiprasad Devkota, tr. David Rubin 1980

Literature of the Hundred Flowers, vol. 1: *Criticism and Polemics*, ed. Hualing Nieh 1981

Literature of the Hundred Flowers, vol. 2: *Poetry and Fiction*, ed. Hualing Nieh 1981

Modern Chinese Stories and Novellas, 1919–1949, ed. Joseph S. M. Lau, C. T. Hsia, and Leo Ou-fan Lee. Also in paperback ed. 1984

A View by the Sea, by Yasuoka Shōtarō, tr. Kären Wigen Lewis 1984

Other Worlds: Arishima Takeo and the Bounds of Modern Japanese Fiction, by Paul Anderer 1984

Selected Poems of Sŏ Chŏngju, tr. with introduction by David R. Mc-
  Cann 1989
The Sting of Life: Four Contemporary Japanese Novelists, by Van C.
  Gessel 1989
Stories of Osaka Life, by Oda Sakunosuke, tr. Burton Watson 1990
The Bodhisattva, or Samantabhadra, by Ishikawa Jun, tr. with intro-
  duction by William Jefferson Tyler 1990
The Travels of Lao Ts'an, by Liu T'ieh-yün, tr. Harold Shadick. Morn-
  ingside ed. 1990
Three Plays by Kōbō Abe, tr. with introduction by Donald Keene 1993
The Columbia Anthology of Modern Chinese Literature, ed. Joseph S.
  M. Lau and Howard Goldblatt 1995
Modern Japanese Tanka, ed. and tr. by Makoto Ueda 1996
Masaoka Shiki: Selected Poems, ed. and tr. by Burton Watson 1997
*Writing Women in Modern China: An Anthology of Women's Literature
  from the Early Twentieth Century*, ed. and tr. by Amy D. Dooling
  and Kristina M. Torgeson 1998
American Stories, by Nagai Kafū, tr. Mitsuko Iriye 2000
The Paper Door and Other Stories, by Shiga Naoya, tr. Lane Dunlop
  2001
Grass for My Pillow, by Saiichi Maruya, tr. Dennis Keene 2002

Studies in Asian Culture

*The Ōnin War: History of Its Origins and Background, with a Selective
  Translation of the Chronicle of Ōnin*, by H. Paul Varley 1967
Chinese Government in Ming Times: Seven Studies, ed. Charles O.
  Hucker 1969
The Actors' Analects (Yakusha Rongo), ed. and tr. by Charles J. Dunn
  and Bungō Torigoe 1969
Self and Society in Ming Thought, by Wm. Theodore de Bary and the
  Conference on Ming Thought. Also in paperback ed. 1970
A History of Islamic Philosophy, by Majid Fakhry, 2d ed. 1983
Phantasies of a Love Thief: The Caurapañcāśikā Attributed to Bilhaṇa,
  by Barbara Stoler Miller 1971

Iqbal: Poet-Philosopher of Pakistan, ed. Hafeez Malik 1971

The Golden Tradition: An Anthology of Urdu Poetry, ed. and tr. Ahmed Ali. Also in paperback ed. 1973

Conquerors and Confucians: Aspects of Political Change in Late Yüan China, by John W. Dardess 1973

The Unfolding of Neo-Confucianism, by Wm. Theodore de Bary and the Conference on Seventeenth-Century Chinese Thought. Also in paperback ed. 1975

To Acquire Wisdom: The Way of Wang Yang-ming, by Julia Ching 1976

Gods, Priests, and Warriors: The Bhṛgus of the Mahābhārata, by Robert P. Goldman 1977

Mei Yao-ch'en and the Development of Early Sung Poetry, by Jonathan Chaves 1976

The Legend of Semimaru, Blind Musician of Japan, by Susan Matisoff 1977

Sir Sayyid Ahmad Khan and Muslim Modernization in India and Pakistan, by Hafeez Malik 1980

The Khilafat Movement: Religious Symbolism and Political Mobilization in India, by Gail Minault 1982

The World of K'ung Shang-jen: A Man of Letters in Early Ch'ing China, by Richard Strassberg 1983

The Lotus Boat: The Origins of Chinese Tz'u Poetry in T'ang Popular Culture, by Marsha L. Wagner 1984

Expressions of Self in Chinese Literature, ed. Robert E. Hegel and Richard C. Hessney 1985

Songs for the Bride: Women's Voices and Wedding Rites of Rural India, by W. G. Archer; ed. Barbara Stoler Miller and Mildred Archer 1986

The Confucian Kingship in Korea: Yŏngjo and the Politics of Sagacity, by JaHyun Kim Haboush 1988

Companions to Asian Studies

Approaches to the Oriental Classics, ed. Wm. Theodore de Bary 1959

Early Chinese Literature, by Burton Watson. Also in paperback ed. 1962

Approaches to Asian Civilizations, ed. Wm. Theodore de Bary and Ainslie T. Embree 1964

The Classic Chinese Novel: A Critical Introduction, by C. T. Hsia. Also in paperback ed. 1968

Chinese Lyricism: Shih Poetry from the Second to the Twelfth Century, tr. Burton Watson. Also in paperback ed. 1971

A Syllabus of Indian Civilization, by Leonard A. Gordon and Barbara Stoler Miller 1971

Twentieth-Century Chinese Stories, ed. C. T. Hsia and Joseph S. M. Lau. Also in paperback ed. 1971

A Syllabus of Chinese Civilization, by J. Mason Gentzler, 2d ed. 1972

A Syllabus of Japanese Civilization, by H. Paul Varley, 2d ed. 1972

An Introduction to Chinese Civilization, ed. John Meskill, with the assistance of J. Mason Gentzler 1973

An Introduction to Japanese Civilization, ed. Arthur E. Tiedemann 1974

Ukifune: Love in the Tale of Genji, ed. Andrew Pekarik 1982

The Pleasures of Japanese Literature, by Donald Keene 1988

A Guide to Oriental Classics, ed. Wm. Theodore de Bary and Ainslie T. Embree; 3d edition ed. Amy Vladeck Heinrich, 2 vols. 1989

Introduction to Asian Civilizations
Wm. Theodore de Bary, General Editor

Sources of Japanese Tradition, 1958; paperback ed., 2 vols., 1964. 2d ed., vol. 1, 2001, compiled by Wm. Theodore de Bary, Donald Keene, George Tanabe, and Paul Varley

Sources of Indian Tradition, 1958; paperback ed., 2 vols., 1964. 2d ed., 2 vols., 1988

Sources of Chinese Tradition, 1960, paperback ed., 2 vols., 1964. 2d ed., vol. 1, 1999, compiled by Wm. Theodore de Bary and Irene Bloom; vol. 2, 2000, compiled by Wm. Theodore de Bary and Richard Lufrano

Sources of Korean Tradition, 1997; 2 vols., vol. 1, 1997, compiled by Peter H. Lee and Wm. Theodore de Bary; vol. 2, 2001, compiled by Yŏngho Ch'oe, Peter H. Lee, and Wm. Theodore de Bary

Neo-Confucian Studies

Instructions for Practical Living and Other Neo-Confucian Writings by Wang Yang-ming, tr. Wing-tsit Chan 1963

Reflections on Things at Hand: The Neo-Confucian Anthology, comp. Chu Hsi and Lü Tsu-ch'ien, tr. Wing-tsit Chan 1967

Self and Society in Ming Thought, by Wm. Theodore de Bary and the Conference on Ming Thought. Also in paperback ed. 1970

The Unfolding of Neo-Confucianism, by Wm. Theodore de Bary and the Conference on Seventeenth-Century Chinese Thought. Also in paperback ed. 1975

Principle and Practicality: Essays in Neo-Confucianism and Practical Learning, ed. Wm. Theodore de Bary and Irene Bloom. Also in paperback ed. 1979

The Syncretic Religion of Lin Chao-en, by Judith A. Berling 1980

The Renewal of Buddhism in China: Chu-hung and the Late Ming Synthesis, by Chün-fang Yü 1981

Neo-Confucian Orthodoxy and the Learning of the Mind-and-Heart, by Wm. Theodore de Bary 1981

Yüan Thought: Chinese Thought and Religion Under the Mongols, ed. Hok-lam Chan and Wm. Theodore de Bary 1982

The Liberal Tradition in China, by Wm. Theodore de Bary 1983

The Development and Decline of Chinese Cosmology, by John B. Henderson 1984

The Rise of Neo-Confucianism in Korea, by Wm. Theodore de Bary and JaHyun Kim Haboush 1985

Chiao Hung and the Restructuring of Neo-Confucianism in Late Ming, by Edward T. Ch'ien 1985

Neo-Confucian Terms Explained: Pei-hsi tzu-i, by Ch'en Ch'un, ed. and trans. Wing-tsit Chan 1986

Knowledge Painfully Acquired: K'un-chih chi, by Lo Ch'in-shun, ed. and trans. Irene Bloom 1987

To Become a Sage: The Ten Diagrams on Sage Learning, by Yi T'oegye, ed. and trans. Michael C. Kalton 1988

The Message of the Mind in Neo-Confucian Thought, by Wm. Theodore de Bary 1989